By the President of the United States of America

A Proclamation
[No. 876 – July 12, 1909 – 36 Stat. 2497]

WHEREAS, certain natural caves, known as the Oregon Caves, which are situated upon unsurveyed land within the Siskiyou National Forest in the State of Oregon, are of unusual scientific interest and importance, and it appears that the public interests will be promoted by reserving these caves with as much land as may be necessary for the proper protection thereof, as a National Monument;

NOW THEREFORE, I, William Howard Taft, President of the United States of America, by virtue of the power in me vested by section two of the Act of Congress, approved June eighth, nineteen hundred and six, entitled, "An Act for the preservation of American antiquities," do proclaim that there are hereby reserved from all forms of appropriation under the public land laws, subject to all prior valid adverse claims, and set apart as a National Monument, all tracts of land in the State of Oregon shown as the Oregon Caves National Monument on the diagram forming a part hereof.

The reservation made by this proclamation is not intended to prevent the use of the lands for National Forest purposes under the proclamations and Executive Order establishing the Siskiyou National Forest, but the two reservations shall both be effective on the land withdrawn, but the National Monument hereby established shall be the dominant reservation, and any use of the land which interferes with its preservation or protection as a National Monument is hereby forbidden.

Warning is hereby given to all unauthorized persons not to appropriate, injure, remove, or destroy any feature of this National Monument, or to locate or settle on any of the lands reserved by this proclamation.

IN WITNESS WHEREOF, I have hereunto set my hand and caused the seal of the United States to be affixed.

DONE At the City of Washington this 12th day of July in the year of our Lord one thousand nine hundred and nine, and of the Independence of the United States the one hundred and thirty-fourth.

[SEAL]

WM. H. TAFT.

By the President:
P. C. KNOX,
Secretary of State

The spectacular Oregon Caves

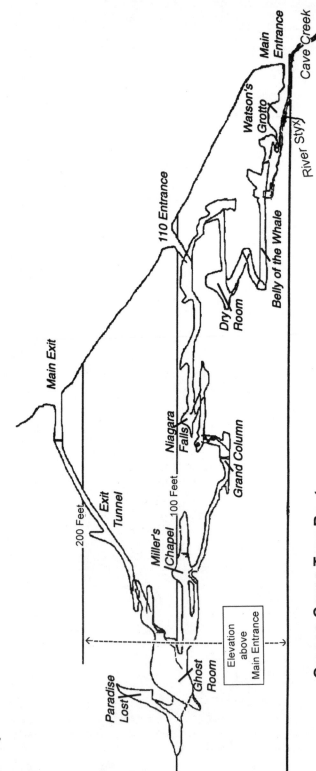

Oregon Caves Tour Route
—Side View—

Cave Creek

River Styx

Main Entrance

Watson's Grotto

Belly of the Whale

Dry Room

110 Entrance

Niagara Falls

Grand Column

Main Exit

Exit Tunnel

Miller's Chapel

100 Feet

200 Feet

Elevation above Main Entrance

Ghost Room

Paradise Lost

Awesome Caverns of Marble in the
Oregon Caves
National Monument –Documentary–
Bert and Margie Webber

WEBB RESEARCH GROUP PUBLISHERS
Books About the Oregon Country

Copyright © Bert Webber 1998
All Rights Reserved Under
Berne Copyright Convention
Printed in Oregon USA

551.44709195
WEB

Please Direct All Inquiries to the Publisher:
WEBB RESEARCH GROUP PUBLISHERS
P. O. Box 314
Medford, Oregon 97501

Material in Appendix G (Geology) is based on an unpublished
informational booklet that is provided to the cave guides
from which the guides prepare their talks.

Library of Congress Cataloging-in-Publication Data

Webber, Bert.
    Awesome caverns of marble in the Oregon Caves National
Monument : documentary / Bert and Margie Webber.
      p.   cm.
    Includes bibliographical references and index.
    ISBN 0-936738-94-4
    1. Caves—Oregon. 2. Oregon Caves National Monument
(Or.) 3. Oregon—History. I. Webber, Margie. II. Title
GB605.07W42 1998   98-4129
551.44.7.0979525 — dc21   CIP

Alternative subject headings:
    Speleology.
    Geology, *see under for sub-divisions*

Contents

Proclamation of the President   1

Introduction   9

1. Early Exploring in the Oregon Caves (1877)   17

2. The *Examiner* Expeditions of 1891 and 1894
     Introduction to the Articles   25
     1891   Part I.   Another Western Marvel; Discovery of
                 a Cavern in Oregon   27
           Part II   Our Splendid Cavern   43
     1894   Part I   The "EXAMINER'S" Expedition
                 Further Discoveries   49
           Part II   The 1894 "EXAMINER'S" Expedition   63

3. Joaquin Miller on Oregon's Marble Halls or
     Lost in the Caves Twice in the Same Day   75

4. Wildlife Abounds at Oregon Caves National Monument   95

5. Civilian Conservation Corps (CCC)   105

6. Visiting the Oregon Caves Today   109
     A. What to Expect   113
     B. Touring the Caves   121

Appendices
     A. Dr. Thomas Condon, Geologist –
         University of Oregon, Visits Caves   141
     B. Early Days at Oregon Caves - 1885   145
     C. Trip to Josephine County's Limestone Caves;   148
         The Greatest Natural Curiosities of Oregon
     D. The "Christmas" Flood – December 22, 1964   150
     E. Names of Caverns, Rooms, and Other Places
         On Or Near Oregon Caves National Monument   153
     F. Visitor Count – Oregon Caves National Monument   178
     G. Geology: The Creation of a Cave and Formation
         of Marble – Decoratives in the Oregon Caves   181
     H. Timeline — Oregon Caves   192
     I. The Grand Chateau; A Wedding at the Oregon Caves   219

Glossary   226
Bibliography   229
Authors   232
Illustration Credits   233
Index   234

Visitors to the Oregon Caves marvel at the awesome sights

Introduction

It has been suggested that the last unvisited wildernesses on earth are unexplored caves. In caves there is the ultimate wilderness. Caves are places with no noise, no jet trails in the sky as there is no sky, no smelly diesel trucks or busses for there are no roads. Besides caves, and under the sea in a special vessel, the best wilderness still left can only be reached by large organizations with lots of money. For most people, caves remain the last frontier – an in-depth appreciation of nature. Such quietude can deepen us emotionally and spiritually by its peace and sense of renewal.

Almost three miles (over 15,000-feet) of underground access have been mapped in the Oregon Caves to date but how much more remains undiscovered is yet to be learned. The maximum depth so far determined is 400-feet below the entrance. These data are compared with the deepest known cave worldwide which is 5,036-feet deep in the Re'seau Goufre Jean Bernard Cave in France. The longest known cave in the United States is Mammoth Cave in Kentucky presently measured at 335 miles.

One writer claimed in an article in the Grants Pass *Courier* on March 16, 1913, that the Oregon Caves, all caverns and access routes combined, were nine miles long – perhaps an over enthusiastic assessment.

The Oregon Caves are at the 4,000-foot elevation on the northwest side of Mount Elijah (6,390 ft elev.). The plural form "caves" applies because there are at least eleven caves in the complex, some connected naturally and some by man-made passageways. There are three sites so far discovered or constructed to enter or exit the various caverns from the outside.

Names Used for the Caves

<u>First known name</u>: "Elijah's Cave."
Although referred to as "Josephine county cave" in William W. Fiddler's "Letter to the Editor" on page 1 of the *Morning Oregonian* August 1, 1877, the writer declares later in his letter, "We named the cave, in honor of the finder, "Elijah's Cave." (See Chapter 1 of this book.) This 1877 narrative appears to be the first newspaper article to mention the caves.

<u>Second known name</u>: "Great Limestone Caves"
An advertisement for the caves appeared in the Rogue River *Courier* on July 9, 1886 identifying the site as the "Great Limestone Caves." The Rogue River *Courier* was an early name for the Grants Pass *Courier*.

<u>Third known name</u>: "Great Oregon Caves"
A writer, George M. Weister, in an article in the February 1902 *The Pacific Monthly,* used the name "Great Oregon Caves"

<u>Fourth known name</u>: "Marble Halls of Oregon"
Joaquin Miller, writing in the September 1909 issue of *Sunset* magazine about his 1907 visit, called the caves the "Marble Halls of Oregon."
Chandler B. Watson wrote in the Rogue River *Courier* on December 17, 1909 of "The Prehistoric Siskiyou Island and the Marble Halls of Oregon." The article related to his August 1907 trip to the caves with Miller.

<u>Fifth known name</u>: "Oregon Caves"
The phrase " Oregon Caves" appears in the 1909 presidential proclamation creating the Oregon Caves National Monument. For the proclamation see page 1 of this book.

<u>Sixth known name</u>: "Josephine County Caves"
This name appears in a promotional brochure which is reported in the 1915 book *Josephine County Caves.*

<u>Alternate name</u>: "Oregon Cave"
On an unknown date in the early 1900's, the name "Oregon Cave" came briefly into use when it was realized that the two entrances were part of the same cave. However, with later explorations, it was determined there are at least eleven caves in the National Monument therefore the name "Oregon Cave" did not survive.

Getting to the Oregon Caves National Monument

Early route to the caves: West from Jacksonville to Williams, then up West Fork Williams Creek to the divide, then down Grayback Creek to Sucker Creek, then hike up the mountain following Logan (after 1913 renamed Cave) Creek to cave. A shortcut was developed to "round" Grayback Mountain near the caves' elevation thereby eliminating the need for the long hike downhill to Sucker Creek then having to hike the creeks upstream to the caves.

Later route: From Grants Pass southeast up the Applegate River to vicinity of Provolt then south to Williams and join the other route from Jacksonville.

Another route: From Grants Pass south to Kerbyville then to Holland then up Sucker Creek to Logan Creek to caves.

Another later route: From Grants Pass south to Kerbyville (Kerby) to vicinity present Cave Junction (before 1926 sometimes called "Cave Station" to confluence of Illinois River and Sucker Creek. Then Sucker Creek to Logan Creek to caves.

Today's roads from Medford and Jacksonville: Take Highway 238 to Wilderville and nearby junction with Highway 199. Go south on 199 to Cave Junction, then east on Highway 46 to end of road at the caves. *

Today's road from Grants Pass: Follow Redwood Highway 199 to Cave Junction, then east on Highway 46 to caves.

> **The obligation of the National Monument, a part of the National Park Service since 1934, earlier administered by the Siskiyou National Forest, has been oriented to preservation and recreation. The Oregon Caves, and $165,446 of Forest Service developments and improvements, was transferred to the National Parks Service on April 1, 1934**

From Crescent City, California: Leave Highway 101 and follow Highway 199 to Cave Junction, then turn east into High-

---

* The authors are familiar with a road having traveled it from Williams over a shoulder of Grayback Mountain to Grayback Campground which is on Caves Highway 46. This route, on BLM, Forest Service and private land, is about forty miles shorter from Medford. (Not suitable for RVs or campers or trailers.) Due to one 15 percent grade, narrow twists, and summer dust, the driving time is about the same as via Grants Pass and Cave Junction. Road not passable in winter. Road not recommended any time.

way 46 to end of road at the caves.

The earliest report about the caves printed in a newspaper the authors have found, is a long "Letter to the Editor" that appeared on page 1 in *Morning Oregonian* on August 1, 1877. The account of this eye-opening visit to the caves is in this book as Chapter 1.

It appears that most early visitors to the caves probably did not make notes but a few of them wrote from memory in later years. Therefore, care must be taken in reading about some early junkets to the caves, routes taken through the caves, and who were actually on these trips. Two of the best descriptions of these early explorations were made by newspaper reporters from San Francisco.

Charles Michelson and F. B. Millard were what today would be called "investigative reporters" who worked for the San Francisco *Examiner*. Michelsen produced the first of these masterpieces of revelations about the caves. His feature articles were serialized on July 11 and 12, 1891 which were the Saturday and Sunday editions. These were the days when newspapers were sold mostly by vendors on busy street corners but as downtown streets had little activity on Sundays, Sunday sales were minimal. Therefore, regrettably, Part II had considerably less readership than Part I. It is also true that good stories can be lost under non-descriptive headlines. Mere labels on stories were the style of the day thus, Michelsen's excellent writing appeared under the ho-hum labels "Another Western Marvel" followed by "Our Splendid Cavern."

The *Examiner's* publisher, William Randolph Hearst, loved action and decided to update the story. He also got better circulation by printing it on better days. But whatever his reasons, in the spring of 1894, he sponsored a full-fledged expedition to the caves by sending a reporter an artist, and a photographer as well as laborers, to explore the caves in great detail. Millard's article, also serialized over two issues, this time hit the streets on Friday and Saturday, May 25 and 26, 1894.

So our readers will have detailed word-pictures of the caves as revealed by these early explorers, we have stayed as close to these original articles as possible, allowing for blurred microfilm and other considerations. Our careful adaptations of these long articles, with copies of the artist's original sketches, appear as Chapter 2 of this book.

The River Styx of the Oregon Caves is often mentioned in reports and in articles about the caves. The name "Styx" comes from Greek mythology and is identified as one of the rivers of the underworld. Most encyclopedias delve into this mythology. The River Styx in the Oregon Caves is of the "underworld," i.e., below the surface of the earth noting that the stream carries that name while underground, but is known as Cave Creek (since 1913) once it emerges. In 1907 the stream was called by Watson the "Stygian," meaning being characteristic of the mythological River Styx's infernal regions – dark or gloomy. The name "Styx" was first applied to the stream in the Oregon Caves in Joaquin Miller's *Sunset* magazine article that appeared in 1909.

This book, a documentary, tells of the conditions found by some early visitors to the caves, includes some of the major cave explorations, takes today's readers along the visitors' tour route and mentions the continuing methods of preserving the caves. In the "Timeline" part of this book are detailed events listed in chronological order.

There is no shortage of "background" reading for scholars, who wish to study the caves and operations there, for the National Park Service's total reading list of many popular articles, government reports, and official correspondence takes more than ninety pages. We have constructed a popular yet effective bibliography from this and other sources that takes much fewer pages.

Writing projects such as ours on the Oregon Caves require many years of accumulating material, being attentive to the subject whenever it comes up, reading "tons of stuff," as well as the assistance of very many people.

We are pleased to have made the acquaintance of John Roth, Resource Management Specialist, Oregon Caves National Monument. Roth and Jay Swofford compiled a list of names of places used throughout the caves which helped us make our list for this book. Roth and Steve Marks compiled a treatise *Oregon*

Chandler Bruer Watson

It is fascinating to note the steps toward establishing the Oregon Caves as a National Monument. Chandler B. Watson was a lawyer, judge, amateur geologist and a member of the Oregon Conservation Commission.

The first chamber in the cave, Watson's Grotto, has been named for him. He was part of the John Kincaid, Joaquin Miller, Chandler B. Watson exploring party of 1907.

Watson called attention of the Commission to the grandeur of the Josephine County Caves and asked that steps be taken to preserve and keep them in their original beauty as a national monument. The Commission urge its representative in Washington, D.C. to talk with Gifford Pinchot, Chief Forester of the U. S. Forest Service. Pinchot went to President Taft and convinced the president to proclaim, through the Antiquities Act, that had been approved merely five weeks earlier, the Oregon Caves as a National Monument on July 12, 1909. The oversight of the new National Monument went to the Forest Service and remained in that jurisdiction until the monument was reassigned to the National Park Service on April 1, 1934.

Elijah Davidson, cave discoverer, and Chandler B. Watson, geologist-preservationist, are memorialized as the leading individuals who found then preserved the Oregon Caves for today's visitors.

Caves National Monument and Roth provided a copy to us. With his kind permission, we have incorporated a part of it here in Chapter 6B "Touring the Oregon Caves." We are also indebted to Roth for willingly providing basic reference information, and some pictures he had accumulated over the years based on his study and first-hand experiences. We thank him generously. Illustration credits for this book are on page 233.

Jason Unger, a Certified Tour Guide in 1997, Oregon Caves Company, led a group of visitors of which we were part, on one of our picture-making expeditions in the cave on November 8, 1997. We appreciate his knowledge about the cave and suggestions for camera angles.

Rose M. Scott, Josephine County Historical Society, Grants Pass, willingly opened her files to us, as did Carol Harbison-Samuelson, Southern Oregon Historical Society, Medford.

Norman D. VanManen assists us in many ways and was our spelunking companion for the expedition mentioned.

We are grateful for the interest and help of Dick Gordon who was a guide at the Oregon Caves during his college years. It was at the caves where he met his wife to be, Kathy, who also worked there.

A great thank you to Omar "Slug" Palmer, 90, who spent many years with the early Oregon Caves Company and treated us to stories of early operations. He and his wife, Constance "Connie" Baker, were married in the Chateau in 1934 a month before the lodge opened to the public. Sam Baker, her father, was President of the Oregon Caves Company and had obtained the first concession license from the Forest Service in 1924. He hosted the wedding and reception putting up all of the guests in rooms of the new building. "Slug" related that there were two reasons for the wedding being at the Chateau. These were to celebrate the construction of this grand six-story hotel in the wilderness, and the fact no church in Grants Pass was large enough to hold all the guests.

We appreciate the input from Harry Christianson who was manager at the concession when the Christmas flood of 1964 inundated the property.

There is no way, this writer believes, for clean documenta-

**The Chateau snowed in for the winter.
In early days when carpenters complained about being snowed in, a message came back that if they wanted to get out, "build skis." They did.**

tion to occur without the help of professional Reference Librarians. For this assistance to our research we are indebted to the staff of the Jackson County Library Service, Ronnie Lee Budge, Director, Medford.

Once this book was put together, we are truly appreciative of the keen eyes and red pencil wielding fingers of Norm Van Manen and Wesley Cretney who did final readings for those every elusive typos.

We are indebted to friendly and helpful folks as all of these, and others, who have assisted to make this book a success. We thanked each of them individually, and now we do so collectively in these pages.

Constructive comments about this book can be sent to us in care of the publisher whose address will be found on page *vi,* but it may be that every letter cannot be personally acknowledged.

Bert and Margie Webber
Central Point, Oregon
Spring 1998

Chapter 1
Early Exploration in the Oregon Caves

———

Transcribed from microfilm *Morning Oregonian* August 1, 1877

Josephine County Cave

———

WILLIAMS CREEK, JOSEPHINE COUNTY, JULY 26. —
TO THE EDITOR OF THE OREGONIAN:

Having just returned from a visit to one of Southern Oregon's great natural wonders, I hasten to send you a brief description of the same.

Two years ago, Mr. E. J. Davidson, one of the most adventuresome and successful mountaineers and hunters of this region, while in pursuit of a deer he had wounded and was following with his dog, accidentally stumbled upon the discovery of what he took to be the mouth of a cave, and which conjecture has since proven to be correct. The discovery was made on the spur of a mountain familiarly known out here as "Old Grayback," and on the side that is drained off toward Sucker Creek or Illinois River. It was not till July 5, 1877, however, that an attempt at exploration of this subterranean cavern was made. Then the discoverer, in company with his brother, Carter Davidson and James Neil, undertook to penetrate its mysterious and marvelously beautiful apartments. Aided by pitch light they were able to penetrate only two or three of the most accessible chambers, which intensified without satisfying their curiosity; but their supply of illuminating material having become exhausted they were compelled to desist. It was on the strength of the report made by these parties, and at the desire of the discoverer of the cave, that, in company with a party of ladies and gentlemen of Williams Creek, the undersigned visited this spot where "nature thrones sublimity" in glistening, if not in

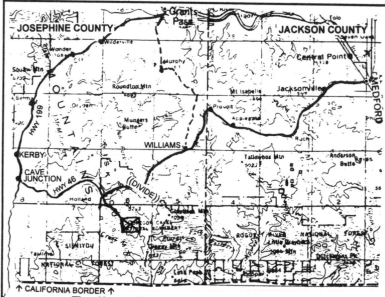

Earliest Directions to the Caves

Based on extracts from descriptive narratives applied to current U.S. Forest Service maps, three probable routes to the Oregon Caves from the earliest times were:

1.) Elijah Davidson left his cabin near the headwaters of West Fork of Williams Creek. He followed the creek upstream to the divide, then down Grayback Creek to a point where he went in a southerly direction "cross-country" to the cave. Later parties leaving Jacksonville (Medford was not founded until 1883), probably followed Grayback Creek to its confluence with Sucker Creek which flows from the south. Logan Creek (in 1913 renamed Cave Creek), joins Sucker Creek in the vicinity of the confluence with Grayback Creek. By following Logan Creek east, a party would arrive at the cave.

2.) Leaving Grants Pass, a party could proceed south to the site of present Murphy on the Applegate River, then continue upstream to the meadow west of Provolt. Leaving the river, the party passed the settlement of Williams following West Fork of Williams Creek as did Davidson earlier.

3.) An early wagon road from Grants Pass went into California by way of Kerby and the later junction for the road (now Cave Junction) to the caves. Early parties passed through Kerbyville along the Illinois River to the confluence of Sucker Creek. Turning east, explorers followed the creeks to the cave.

Today's Oregon Highway 46 leaves Highway 199 at Cave Junction and runs generally east for 20 miles to the caves.

Elijah Davidson as a young man

"icy halls." But to describe the trip fully, I had best to commence with the commencement.

Our party consisted at the start of but six, to wit: Miss Endora A. Godfrey, Miss Margaret Davidson, of Portland; Mr. Julius Goodwin, two boys and this deponent. We traveled up the right-hand fork of Williams Creek to its head, thence across one or two streams that run westerly into Sucker Creek, then up a large mountain that puts out from Gray Back to the milk ranch of Messrs. Goodwin and Davidson. Here we camped for the night and partook of the kind hospitality of these certainly highly elevated and obliging dairymen. The next morning our party was increased by the addition to our numbers of Mrs. Julius Goodwin, Mr. Frank Rose, and E. J. Davidson. Of our party were, also, two young lads, named David John Jr. and Ira Sparlin. To the place we wished to reach was only about one and one-half miles from the milk ranch, but owing to the ruggedness of the route and the course we took to get there, we were fully three hours in reaching it with our riding animals. Soon after we reached the scene of operations, however, the work of exploration began and was entered upon by each member of our party with a zeal and enthusiasm that meant business. From the mouth of the cave emerges a branch of water, and it is up the bed of this stream we first begin our underground perambulations. The mountain is of limestone formation, and the caverns and cross-caverns, in almost every form imaginable and unimaginable, which we beheld with delightful amazement, were evidently the result of the action of water. After penetrating perhaps one hundred yards, we leave the stream to examine upper and side rooms that do not require so much exposure of the feet to water. Every

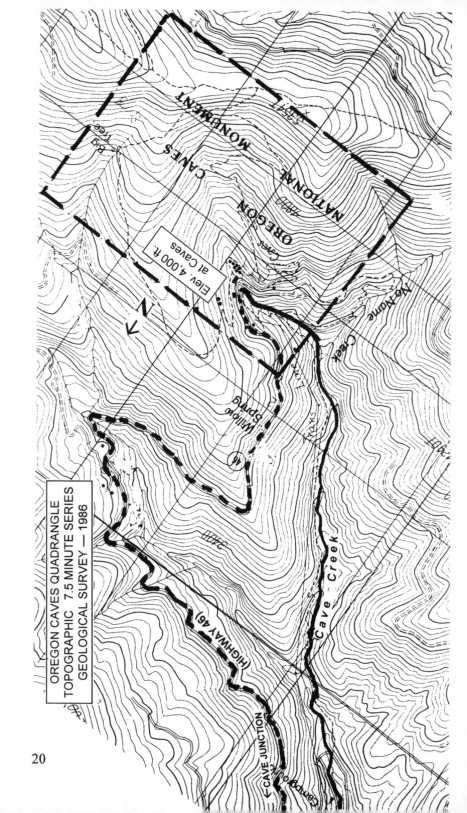

OREGON CAVES QUADRANGLE
TOPOGRAPHIC 7.5 MINUTE SERIES
GEOLOGICAL SURVEY — 1986

OREGON CAVES NATIONAL MONUMENT

Elev. 4,000 ft.
at caves

Big Tree

N

Willow Spring

(HIGHWAY 46)

Cave Creek

No Name Creek

CAVE JUNCTION

20

**Signatures on cave wall from 1877 include
Carter Davidson and Dora (Endora) Godfrey.**

successive department reached, evoked from each and every member such vociferfera-tive expressions as "Oh, Oh, Oh, Isn't it nice, isn't [it] beautiful, etc," and one of the earliest convictions that overcame us most completely was that it would be impossible for us in the short period of our stay to do anything like justice to the examination of these diversified, fantastic and indescribable realms of the underworld.

Prentice's ode to Mammoth Cave has now a much clearer meaning:

Crystal Founts

Almost invisible in their serene
And our transparency – high pillared domes
With stars and flowers all fretted like the halls
Of Oriental monarchs

...are expressions admirable suited to a description of this Josephine County cave. The stalagmite and stalactite formations

21

Belly-squirming one's way through tight spaces was the common method one employed to get through many of the passages in the Oregon Caves in the early days, and continues to the present time when National Park Service Rangers explore and map parts of the cave not accessible to the public. (ABOVE) Helen Scully, NPS in a crawl space in North Canyon Passage Extension in 1993. (RIGHT PAGE) NPS Ranger Steve Knutson. He and Scully were partners for this research trip.

of this cave surpassed anything ever dreamed of in the sphere of Arts, and nothing I ever beheld in Nature before, so completely overcame me with suggestions of sublimity and beauty.

In some places the floor was almost as smooth as polished marble, and in others the ceiling is frescoed all over with bright crystals or stalactite, in the shape and resembling icicles. In one chamber in particular, which we casually designated The King's Palace, was this the case. The various members of the party commenced here, in obedience to a very natural impulse, to break off specimens to bring away with them, but in obedience to a suggestion that it looked like a shame to desecrate or deface anything in nature so beautiful as that was, they readily ceased the work of spoliation; and let us hope that future tourists and adventurers will be governed by the same honorable deference

and spare this apartment if none of the others.

A volume might be written descriptive of the beauties of the small portion we beheld, which portion did not comprise one-tenth perhaps not one ten-thousandth – part of these

"Dim and Awful Aisles."

One great danger to be constantly guarded against is that of getting lost. Frequently we lost our way and got into narrow crevices through which we could see a light in some lower apartment, but could not reach it without retracing our steps and finding some larger crevice. What could be explored by enlarging some of these narrow fissures is a matter of conjecture. The furthest back any of our party got was perhaps not over 400 yards. To make that distance through its various angles, dips and ascents, required nearly an hour's travel after we were familiar with the route. We did not try to follow up the main stream of water, which undoubtedly constitutes the main part of the cave, but have left lots of work for future explorers. Our party obtained many beautiful and valuable specimens as souvenirs of the very hard and – for the ladies – dangerous journey. Many of the prettiest things however were spoiled in breaking them off. Some were like a mule's ear in shape only three or four times as

Carbide lantern

large and in places perfectly transparent. The ears of many of the animals were represented on the walls, together with many varieties of sea shells: and then again clusters of grape, flowers and many varieties of vegetables. These attractions, though, will rapidly disappear as the place becomes frequented by visitors.

We named the cave, in honor of the finder, "Elijah's Cave." It is situated in the southern part of the county, about 15 miles southwest of Williamsburg,* or say 37 miles in the same direction from Jacksonville. A better route than the one we traveled can probably be found, when sightseers can reach the cave without roughing it as we did. It is a sight however, well worth many times the trouble we encountered in reaching it, to anyone who has a particle of admiration for the sublime and beautiful. Yea, "beautiful are all the thousand snow-white gems that lie in these mysterious chambers."

—Wm. W. Fidler

---

* Williamsburg was a pioneer community of several hundred people on a rise in the ground about three miles southwest of Provolt and about three miles northeast of present Williams. The community was a little east of the present highway from Grants Pass to Williams. There was a post office "Williamsburg" from Nov. 16, 1860 but it lasted only until July 5, 1861. There may be more confusion noting there was also a post office "Williams Creek" in Jackson County, just across the county line from Williams in Josephine County (and about one mile upstream from Provolt). The three, according to McArthur and Helbock were never in the same place.

Chapter 2

The *Examiner* Expeditions of 1891 and 1894

Introduction to the Articles

William Randolph Hearst loved to sell newspapers and as publisher of the San Francisco *Examiner,* he was constantly on the lookout for good stories. He knew that the more sensational his topics, the more papers he could sell. Among many subjects in which he became interested is what is now known as the Oregon Caves National Monument.

It could be that Hearst, a well-read adventurer in his own right, may have taken a page from the activities of Henry M. Stanley who a few years earlier, as a newspaper reporter, explored Central Africa to, among other things, search for and find the Scottish missionary Dr. David Livingston. That safari, in 1874 to 1877, was sponsored in a joint effort by newspapers, The London *Daily Telegraph* and the *New York Herald.* Could Hearst also sponsor an expedition?

Hearst sent a reporter, Charles Michelson, with a photographer, a Mr. Worthington, to the cave in the summer of 1891 to learn what that "Josephine County Cave" was all about. The newspaper's project became a major undertaking.

Reporter Michelson turned out a major feature article that excited thousands of readers and brought good publicity to the cave. Although access to the cave at that time was very limited, a few people were physically hardy enough, and had the time and money, to make a visit.

About three years later, on invitation of the Oregon Caves Improvement Company, Hearst decided on a second expedition.

San Francisco Exam

(The Oregon Cave Improvement Company appears to have participated in the venture but to what extent, other than providing a cabin, has not been determined.)*

These expeditions of 1891 and 1894 to the mountains of Southern Oregon required masterful planning for transport as well as supplies, especially the second visit which was an out-of-the-ordinary enterprise in North America in its day. With these expeditions, publisher Hearst appears to have made the first concerted effort, by a newspaper, to sponsor a team of explorers and laborers, to study and explore the Oregon Caves. His "teams" included expert reporters, photographers, artists and some unidentified laborers. On their return to San Francisco, Hearst provided large amounts of space in his *Examiner* to tell about the caves. Each of the expeditions were featured in serialized fashion. Parts I and II on succeeding days for each trip. He sold a lot of newspapers.

---

* Nothing is mentioned in the *Examiner's* 1894 article about the Oregon Cave Improvement Company

The 1891 Expedition

Another Western Marvel; Discovery of a Cavern in Oregon That Rivals the Mammoth Cave of Kentucky

The "EXAMINER'S" Exploration of Many Miles of Chambers and Corridors Full of Beautiful and Curious Formations; A Week Among the Crevasses; Chasms and Abysses in the Heart of a Great Mountain – The Entrance to the Fissure Discovered by a Hunter Who Chased a Bear – Waterfalls, a Lake, and Running Streams Among the Subterranean Features – Stalactites That Counterfeit Familiar Objects and Make the Passages and Rooms Fantastic.

[CAVE STATION (Or.)], July 11, 1891 — Among the natural wonders of the North American Continent few have excited so profound and mysterious an interest as those vast underground caverns, the Mammoth Cave of Kentucky and the Luray Cavern of Virginia. The discovery that the Pacific Coast possesses a worthy rival of these extraordinary formations will be news of world wide interest. A few weeks ago, it came to the knowledge of the EXAMINER that a cave of unusual dimensions had been discovered just over the California borderline in Oregon. A correspondent and photographer were at once dispatched to the spot. The result of their investigation proves that the first meager reports of the discovery were more than borne out by the facts. The EXAMINER'S correspondent and photographer penetrated the cavern to a distance of five miles, finding the peculiarities of formation which characterize the Mammoth and Luray Caves – stalactites, eroded by the drip into the most grotesque shapes, the stalagmites, forming a strange variety of figures. The exploration of the cave was by no means complete. Though miles of the fantastic underground chambers were traveled over, there remain a large number of passages which could not be followed to their termination in the time available to do so.

Enough has been done, however, to show conclusively that the famous Eastern caverns have a worthy rival in this Western cave. The report of this exploration is given [here over the next two days] and will be found extraordinarily interesting

This major feature article was written by Charles Michelson, a reporter for the San Francisco *Examiner*. (It is cited in the bibliography.) Our resource base is a typewritten then mimeographed transcript from the newspaper, as a microfilm of the original was not available. Our account allows a little license for clarity. Readers are reminded that some of the names of locations in the caves as identified in the article are not on the present tour route through the caves or have been changed. —Editor

Near the head of a great canyon in Southern Oregon there is a great cave. Two openings give access to it. These openings look like small fissures in a big limestone bluff. This limestone extends for miles. It looks as massive and solid outside as any mountain in the world, but is honey-combed like a pile that has been exposed to the teredo for years.

For miles and miles these cracks and crevasses extend, without any apparent order or system. Strike a block of ice with a mallet and the cracks that show inside the transparent block indicate the manner of the faults in the great limestone bluffs.

Many of these passages are of surprising beauty, semi-transparent stalactites, giant milk-white pillars, and pools and dreams of the purest, clearest water in the world make the underground maze a veritable fairyland.

The cave is situated in Josephine County, Oregon about twelve miles north of the California line and about forty miles

Rigors of the Trail

No one had been over this trail for two years or more when the EXAMINER party struck it and the journey up the mountain canyon was very long indeed. Trees had fallen across it and always in the most precipitous places. The axemen ahead had to hew a way through these fallen giants. Where the trunks were too big, they had to clear a new trail around the great fallen trees. It frequently happened that a single big tree blocked our way. While a boy could scramble over it and be on the other side where the trail was clear again, in half-a-minute, yet in such places it took half-an-hour to an hour to make way for the horses and heavily laden pack mules.

The trail zigzags about, to north, south, east and west, but always it goes up, continues up, and up some more, until the traveler is really tired but the rewarding view along the way is grandeur for one can see the peaks of the Coast Range over all the lower and closer ridges.

It is a long trail hard enough to weary even the brawniness of men with the stoutest souls. It was 2:30 o'clock in the afternoon when the expedition started up the trail and it was 9 o'clock at night before the shout of the first man up apprised the exhausted stragglers, strung out for half-a-mile behind him, that he had found the cave. It took six-and-a-half hours to climb to the cave. On accomplishing our goal we took a rest.

from the coast.

There are a number of ways of reaching it, but about the easiest is from Grants Pass on the line of the Oregon and California branch of the Southern Pacific Railroad.

Thirty miles of staging from that point brings you to Kerby, an old town that was a rushing, roaring place when all the creeks and gulches in the vicinity were crowded with placer miners, but which is now a sleepy farming town among the hills and the fir forests. You can travel a dozen or fifteen miles beyond Kerby in a team, but the last half of this is pretty rough.

The route is to the south along the Illinois River until its junction with Sucker Creek, thence, northerly and easterly up Sucker Creek past where Grayback Creek comes in and to the great canyon that runs off to the northeast. Wagons have gone as far as this, but it takes the stoutest horses and the staunchest vehicles to make the trip. The EXAMINER party was forced to leave its wagons and go ahead with a pack train from about four miles below.

Where the big canyon turns off is the skeleton of a ruined

cabin, built nobody knows by whom and nobody remembers when. This is an important landmark. It indicates the point where the real hard work of the trip begins.

The cave is near the head of this canyon and the road to it is a narrow trail, steep and wearying. For seven or eight miles, this trodden thread leads around rocks, over slippery hillsides, twisting between great trees over, under and around giant trunks and across swift-running streams.

(Coming down it was only a little over two hours from the time the party started from the cave that it reached the skeleton cabin on Sucker Creek. So much for the difference between climbing up an obstructed trail and down a clear one.)

It took two full days for the EXAMINER expedition to reach the cave from Kerby, but that was mainly because the road was so badly obstructed. Now since the trees are cut through and the trail has been made around the bad places, it should be made in a day or at the most a day-and-a-half.

The usual mishaps common to expeditions through an unfrequented country were met on the Terrill. The wagons stuck in the worst part of the creek, and had to be pried up the steep bank. The packs turned over on the mules in the steepest places on the trail in spite of diamond hitches, the animals strayed off when they were turned out to graze. But the expedition got there in good order when it did finally get there.

Half-a-dozen torches – the regular "hurrah for Cleveland-and-Harrison teams" kind – were taken along to illuminate the cave. Five miles of twine sufficed to keep the way along the labyrinthian caverns. These with a camera and enough magnesium flash powder to light up the "Chaos and old Night" constituted the outfit for the explorers.

The main mouth of the cave is a big triangular gap in the face of an enormous limestone bluff. From it there tumbles a roaring, dancing mountain stream* so bright and sparkling that it seems to be laughing with delight at having escaped from the gloomy darkness of that great cave.

---

* This is today called the River Styx when the stream is in the cave, but takes the name Cave Creek once flowing outside the cave.

It was in this hole-in-the-wall that a wounded black bear took refuge and so revealed the cave to the hunter Elijah Davidson.

Mr. Davidson lighted pine boughs and threw them into the black hole and by their light saw his quarry. The next day he returned to explore his find. He left his horse at the foot of the mountain with a note pinned to the saddle telling where he had gone. At the mouth of the cave he left his coat with another note. Then with a fat pine stick for a torch, he plunged inside. He went on and on from one chamber to another for several hundred yards but he found no end. By this time he was chilled through and he decided to postpone further exploration for a day or two. He crawled back in the direction he had come but he could not find daylight again. For four hours he threaded his way through fantastic grottos where no man had trod before. He broke off stalactites and marked where he went so as not to tread the same path twice. And at last, when his pine stick was burning his fingers, he saw a gleam of light and soon he was in the open air again. But his coat was not there! He had come out at another opening a quarter mile from where he went in and he was now higher on the bluff.

Other people heard of the strange cave and went into it until they thought they knew all about it. But every time a more than usually venturesome man got into the rocks, he found another passage leading still farther into the depths.

The cave, or, rather the country around it, for there are no statutes regarding the taking up of caves – is covered by a notice of location of a mineral claim. The locators are W. J. Henderson and F. M. Nickerson of Kerby and a Captain Smith of San Diego.

It was early in the morning of 30th of June when the EXAMINER party was ready to enter the cave. There was a cool morning mountain breeze that still had the chill of the snowy Siskiyous on it. It was a cold morning and yet when the party reached the mouth of the cave, the air outside was warm in comparison with the frigid blast that came out from the opening in the bluff.

This main opening, from which the creek flows, was the

first entered. For a dozen feet only, you could stand upright. The ceiling then got lower and the walls were nearer together then. But, almost doubled over, we pushed on up to our ankles in swiftly flowing water that seemed as cold as ice. Thirty feet from the mouth the daylight was no longer visible. A great boulder caught midway between the walls, made an upper and lower corridor. To the left a great hole gaped and from the right, the floor broke off abruptly in a grinning crack.

The left hand passage was the only one that did not lead in a long series of rooms, and it was the largest opening of the four. Stooping under a great rock that jutted from the wall the first of the party found himself in an octagonal chamber a dozen feet high and as much in diameter. It was a two-story room. Half way to the ceiling a comparatively thin sheet of rock made a ceiling for the lower room and a floor for the upper. There were bones in these rooms – bones of deer and smaller animals and there were other indications there was or had been the den of some flesh-eating beast, probably a bear. There are plenty of bears in this section of the country, fine black fellows, shyer than deer, but also able to make things very disturbing to a hunter who wounds one in the brush.

This double room was the only place in the cave where evidences of animal life were then found. The clear cold waters that ran noiselessly on the floors of some of the corridors or thundered down the walls of others were destitute of inhabitants, though outside, a short distance away from where the creek boils from the mouth of the cave, there are beautiful trout in abundance.

Even the still mysterious lake that was found miles away from the light seemed to hide nothing living. Not a bat or a mouse or even a worm fluttered or crawled in the long tortuous passages.

Of the other openings just inside the mouth of the cave, the two that run ahead – one above and the other below – go on for many miles.

The passage to the right, which went down the gash in the rock, was followed for half-a-mile. It is a succession of high, narrow rooms and small corridors. On the walls, the stalactites and stalagmites have united and formed pillars, thus, making the rooms still narrower. Probably these pillars, which from their size, seem to be among the oldest in the cave, have covered up (grown together) and hidden the openings.

> Some parts of the pillared wall gave back a hollow sound when struck. There are wonders in those hermetically sealed apartments yet to be found probably even more marvelous than those that we have seen.

The last man in the party had in his pocket a ball of twine. One end of this twine was tied fast to a rock at the mouth of the cave, and as they moved forward, the line unwound.

As we clamored through the narrow passages, wondering at their fantastic pendants and projections that looked even more grotesque in the light of flaming torches, we forgot that we were cold, wet and tired. Each step showed something stranger than that which we had passed. Strange shapes and curious irregularities kept the eyes wide open. A lime encrusted boulder covered with fretwork delicate as hoar frost, loomed up against the intense blackness beyond what appeared as an enormous bear's head. There were glistening icicles for the teeth and the whole picture s___. Even while the eye took in the features, they changed and, instead of a fierce black bear's head, there was now only an irregular boulder again.

In the distance where our light barely reached, ugly black arms appeared. More than once our party suddenly halted when one of the spooky beasts moved for in the weird, surreal light, they seemed to move, though closer up they showed as simply openings into other branches of the crevasses.

The most intense silence prevailed in this passage. Not a breath of air was stirring there while in the main corridor which we had just left, the wind rushed through so fiercely that in the straighter passages the flames of the torches struggled and sputtered, but at last were conquered and blown. This left the explorers in darkness so complete that it made the eyes ache. Then there was nothing to do but crawl, each holding to the other until the cessation of the gale told them they were behind a rock or turn where the torches could be relighted.

But this new passage was absolutely still. Even the splutter -

ing of the torches sounded loud and the crunching of the frost-like coating beneath the feet seemed like profanation. Somehow no body cared to talk much and what was said, was said in whispers.

Several very tempting openings were passed, but finally a particularly easy looking door was reached, turning to the right. It was not easy for long. The ceiling rock got closer to the floor, and once again the walls came nearer together. We stooped, and we got to our hands and knees then we went down flat.

So half-a-dozen of us we had to wriggle and squirm along snakewise, our clothing catching on the brittle spikes and the fretted floor tearing at our knees. It was exhausting work for a while, but at last the passage grew wider and presently we were in a room where we could stand upright.

That was a wonderful place. Along either wall ran a low flat bench of rock. In this bench were several depressions as distinct and sharp as though cut with a chisel. These depressions were only an inch or so deep, were perfectly rectangular and perfectly level. They were filled to the brim with water, and the white rock glistened through it beautifully. All around it was dry; no water dripping from above, none welling up from below. These squares of water reflected like looking glasses when the torches were held over them.

The "Mirror Room" this chamber was named and the first photograph in the cave was taken there. Explosion of the flash powder made the air shake, while for an instant every point and corner of the room was plainly visible.

We started to go as the photographer reached for the line. The twine was gone! He only had the [cards] in his pocket. So wonderful and interesting was the road that we never noticed when the line ran out. The end of that cord was somewhere a quarter of a mile or so back in the rock.

We finally found it. If we had not, this article would not have appeared today, but it took nearly two hours scrambling along holes and tunnels that we had not passed on the way in. It was a very uncomfortable two hours. There were no end of passages it seemed and they wound around and above and below one another in the most perplexing and bewildering fashion. We felt very serious and unpleasant before an unexpected slip down the side of a craggy chamber, as big as a ballroom, showed us the thin line of twine.

So we got out. What a relief! We had spent nearly eight hours in the cave.

"What shall we call this branch of the cave," mused the reporter, notebook in hand. The photographer, who can be a humorist when he gets peeved at something, growled, "The Lost Cord." That was the name we gave it.

The air outside was as a blast from an oven. There was a difference of fully forty degrees Fahrenheit between the temperature in the cave and that of the air out of it.

The bright sunshine seemed garish and the great fir trees unreal to the eyes that had that whole day seen nothing but the white lime of stalactites, stalagmites, pillars, and flowstone. We had not noticed the cold of the cave as our physical efforts kept us in a perspiration. Our clothes were white as if we had been fished from a flour bin and we were wet to the skin from the continual droplets that fell from the pointed stalactites.

It was by now evening before we were fed and in trim to try the cave again. This time the hole on the top of the bluff gave us entrance.

For a quarter of a mile there was little difficulty. There was some scrambling over the rocks and clambering up and down ladders that had been placed by the first to venture into the cave as had to be done, but the work of the morning had taught us much about moving about in caves, and the ground was rapidly gone over. After the quarter of a mile however, the troubles began. A great chamber, named the "Dining Room" because of a bench of rock with a level top that occupied one side of the room, and looked more like a table than anything else, was the last of the easy traveling. From there, a chimney barely wide enough to squeeze through went up at an angle of about sixty degrees. It is one of the most difficult places in all the caves, but it is the only way to some of the most wonderful places under the ground. For twenty yards at a time, the only way to move was to clutch the thicker spikes ahead and drag the body along getting scratched and torn by those same spikes as the hapless body was dragged over them. Our clothing was of little protection.

Fortunately, at irregular intervals there were cracks and breaks in the chimney where we could rest ourselves by struggling to our hands and knees. Of course, with the cold water we were wet through every stitch we wore. The work was hard, that is, very hard, but the exercise kept us warm. It was only when we crouched in some opening to rest that our teeth chattered. But always ahead was the dark blotch that showed the corridor still went on and on, and on. One hundred yards of this brought us to large rooms and once again broad passages. No pen can adequately describe the wonders of some of those chambers that had never been seen before.

Rod after rod of stately columns, as regular and clear as freshly sculptured marble pillars, divide the room and increase the mystery of the great maze. Overhead a thousand glistening droplets of water, with the apex of a brilliant white spear head, reflect the light from the glowing torches.

Everywhere on the walls, masses of shining lime, slowly deposited for ages, counterfeited the shapes of well known things.

The Old Man

Turning an abrupt corner of the cavern so high that the torches did not light to the ceiling of the magnificent dome, a great gaunt face sends chills down one's back. You know, of course, that the malevolent eye is only a shadow, the mouth a fault in the gigantic stalactite stained by a drop of iron that somehow has been washed down into the limestone cracks. But the face – the beard alone as long as a man – is uncanny and as long as you can see the visage you have an uncomfortable feeling that the old man, who has been there as long as water and rocks have been, is watching you with no approving glance.

But the photographer planted his camera tripod right beside him and the flash of the powder revealed that the image of the face had been made. The dull report of the magnesium flash reverberated many times for these caves and caverns are great places for echoes.

The "Guardian of the Cave" was, of course, the name of the great visage in the pillar.

As nearly as could be estimated from the amount of string paid out, this curious feature is two and one half miles from the entrance of the cave. At a rough guess, it is 1,000 feet below the roots of the great fir trees that crown this mountain. The caverns are larger after the Guardian is behind us but the paths are rougher.

> There is something exhilarating about this wandering around in the heart of a mountain.
>
> The fact that the falling of a rock as big as one's body into a hole may shut you in there forever to watch the doorway to the inner caverns, along with the "Guardian of the Cave," until the lime charged water shall have changed you too into a strange stalagmite feature of the great cave, makes you indifferent to ordinary danger.

You tread carelessly, and as a matter of course along slimy ledges, while just behind you are black chasms of unknown depths, and somehow the thought of slipping and falling never occurs to you.

A short distance beyond the gigantic face we crossed a long, low room with a floor of broken boulders. Full in the wall at the height of a man's shoulders above the floor was a hole. A torch thrust through showed only blackness beyond. A rock thrown through, it did not strike bottom for three seconds. After consultation, a rope was made fast to a pillar. The other end was tied around the waist of an EXAMINER man, while the photographer let out the rope until the suspended one found a foothold.

Another passage was found and the photographer managed to lower himself to reach a ledge in the side of the enormous well. Once situated, he made a picture. His companion was hanging to a tongue of rock. The main floor of the chamber was a hundred feet below. This place was enchristened the "Giant's Tongue." This formation is quite common throughout the cave. Only a hundred feet inside the entrance is another Giant's Tongue but that one is only a miniature by comparison, about four feet long.

Some ugly climbing brought us to the floor. We counted sixteen archways that led from it and we chose one in which there hung a perfect stocking over twenty feet long. When such a stocking was offered for Santa Claus to fill, there must have been good luck.

The corridors were beautiful and we had seen so much that we hardly noticed them, so on we went for another quarter of a mile. There the string gave out but we still went on trusting to compass and charcoal markings on the walls to find our way back. During the last few hundred yards, we heard the murmur of water that grew louder as we came along. We followed the sound and at last found its source – a splendid waterfall. It was not a big stream, but it leaped thirty feet. It hardly gathered after the fall when it gurgled into a hole and disappeared.

Passing this waterfall was a veritable grove of high pillars confronting us. Through these bars, as though a prison gate, we could barely make out the gleam of water. It took some time to get past those pillars, but when we did we found ourselves in a veritable fairyland.

Before us was a beautiful little lake with a surface as clear as that of a mirror reflecting the tessellated roof – a roof that indeed looked to have been paved in a mosaic pattern of small square blocks. The reflected scene was distorted by the glare of the torches. On every hand glistened the innumerable curious forms that the lime charged water makes. Behind the pillars the waterfall roared. On the other side of the chamber a still larger cataract reached from floor to dome. But this one was still. It was a cataract in stone, perfect in every detail. The water trickling over the rocks during all those years had built it up to what we saw – a waterfall frozen in the midst of its rushing.

Above us were a myriad of bayonet points each tipped with a star, for the drops of water caught the light of our torches and showed us a firmament as glorious as that which shown on the pines half a mile above our heads.

And in the midst of all this grandeur the two men, with their rough solid, torn clothes and their camera, looked as much out of place as a locomotive in a hot house.

We hated to leave the scene but our light began to burn low

and we hurried back to where we left the extra torches.

Day was breaking when we reached the mouth of the cave and wet and exhausted and hungry as we were, we tumbled into our blankets and slept through the day.

> Every day for a week we went as far as we could into the bowels of the mountain, and yet at the end of that time there seemed almost as much yet unexplored as had been already gone over.

The two vertical divisions of the main cave were found exceedingly interesting though hardly as picturesque as the upper cave already described.

The Fourth of July was the final day spent in the cave. On that day the branches of the upper main cavern were taken in succession. Traveling was excessively difficult. There seemed to be more water here than anywhere else. The passages were smaller and rougher than in any other part we visited. It was on this day that the only serious accident to the EXAMINER'S party occurred.

The photographer had just made a picture then he took a few steps forward. Where he stood seemed as solid as the floor of a mine but just as he lifted his torch to better see a particularly curious cluster of stalactites, the floor gave way and he disappeared.

In the fissure he had fallen into, he struck the sides of it several times and finally a great splash told us that he had reached bottom. Peering down, his companions could see nothing but the near-vertical walls of rock projecting shelves that hid the bottom.

"Are you hurt"?

"No," came the first reply from below.

"Are you hurt"? was demanded again.

"Halloo—o—o"!

The man at the bottom could not hear at first but he could shout and shout he did. A torch was lowered to him, his own having gone out and lost during his fall. Another EXAMINER man went back one mile to the entrance to the cave for help. He was soon back with the guide and a long rope the end of which was dropped into the chasm.

"Can you put the rope around you"?

From the depths came the answer, "No – my arms are hurt."

There was only one way to proceed. Somebody had to go down into the hole and help him. The other EXAMINER man fastened the rope under his arms, then dropped and slid and clambered down nearly forty feet. He located his partner, still very dazed from the sudden fall, trying to stand in ice cold water up to his knees. His entire body was soaked. He was badly scratched over much of his body, from which blood was oozing. His clothes had been mostly torn from him. But there were no bones broken. It was a chore to get him out of this hole but with the rope tied about him, and men at the top pulling, he was lifted to safety. The rope went down into the hole a second time to retrieve his partner. The long slow walk out of the cave was painful to everyone. Joyfully, after a two day rest in his blankets, the party was ready to hike down the mountain on the start for home.

The place our photographer, Worthington, fell was named "Beauty's Slide" for the same reason that a particularly tall man is nicknamed "Shorty." That hole had been anything but beautiful however, before this incident many beautiful places had been visited.

Among the most interesting places was a large chamber where the stalactites were more numerous than in any other part of the cavern. There the process of column building could easily be watched. It seemed to be raining in this cave for from every projecting point on the ceiling fell a steady drizzle of water. On the floor, where each drop landed, was a stalagmite – just a round mound at first – but getting higher and higher where the dripping was fastest.

> **But one question would keep suggesting itself. These icicles will all eventually join the mounds and once together will form a column. Every drop of water will thicken these columns until the entire room becomes crowded. As this process continues throughout the whole cave, what will eventually be come of Oregon's new wonder?**

It seemed as if one could see the increase in size as the drops fell, but of course that was imaginary for nature is not that fast at working.

But even if it does fill up, it will not be for a great many years therefore that need not worry the people who will still want to visit the cave.*

At the entrance to the Rainy Cavern is a curious formation. From the middle of the ceiling hangs a great mass of limestone then from either side it looks like an enormous clenched fist so, we call this "Sullivan's Hallway" for the great boxer, John L. Sullivan. Further on, right where the passage turns at a considerable angle, a number of stalactites have formed a very fair elephant's head.

While this account of the exploration takes the various features in succession, it must not be supposed that the route followed was by any means a direct one. There is hardly twenty feet of the entire distance that is in a straight line for the passages twist and intersect in a most confusing fashion.**

Three miles from the caves on the flat that crowns the mountain are a couple of beautiful lakes. Several small streams flow from these lakes but have no apparent outlets. It is supposed that the water from them finds its way into the limestone caverns and that is where all of the streams and waterfalls in the cave originate.

It is idle speculation on the probable extent of the caves. It is certainly five miles in from the mouth for the EXAMINER party went that far. Four miles is a moderate estimate of the width of the cave. As to its depth it can only be said that a torch was lowered nearly 800 yards in one shaft and was hauled up some minutes later still lighted.

It was a hard week's work for the EXAMINER expedition. The men traveled as best they could under stalactites, over stalag-

---

* Charles Michelson wrote these lines in 1891. Now, 107 years later, the cave is still not filled but the water still drips.

** Over the years, as the early guides and later the National Park Service discover new exciting views within the caves which will be enjoyable for visitors to see, the tour routes have been changed. It is presumed that visitor accessible routes will continue to start in the same place and end using the exit tunnel constructed in the 1930's. But the visitor accessible routes between these two sites may change. —Editor

Carrying a small flashlight today is safer, cleaner, non-damaging to the caves, compared to the torches and candles of yesteryear.

mites, around magnificent columns, and the hardest thing about it was that at the end of the week as at the beginning, there was still ahead of the explorers that fascinating black blotch – another opening of another corridor that would lead to yet unvisited caverns. ◇

Our Splendid Cavern

More About the Great Cave in the Northern Siskiyous; Hunting For a Steaming Well; What One Visitor Claims to Have Discovered Somewhere Among the Tortuous Corridors Beyond the Ghost's Hall.

[CAVE STATION (Or.)], July 12, 1891 — The news of the discovery of the great cave in Oregon and the publication yesterday of the results of the EXAMINER'S exploration has started everybody to talking about the cavern.

It transpires that there are quite a number of smaller caves in Oregon and California, but this is the only one yet discovered worthy of rank either in point of extent, or of the beauty of its features with such famous wonders as the Mammoth Cave of Kentucky and the Luray Caverns in Virginia.

Though the new cavern has many features in common with these caves it differs from them in many ways.

The temperature of both the Eastern caves is 54-degrees Fahrenheit. In the Oregon cave it is certainly less than fifty degrees and in some places not more than 45-degrees F.*

The limestone bluff, in which the cavern is located, is only the croppings of a great belt that extends clear through the Siskiyous into California. Most of the creeks in the vicinity yielded rich returns to the placer miners years ago. The country is full of quartz.

Chambers and Corridors

Though there is no real order to the subterranean corridors and chambers. The EXAMINER'S party found that there were really three main divisions or series, to the cave. There are pas-

---

* The temperature on November 8, 1997 when the editors were in the caves was 41-degrees F. —Editor

sages connecting them, but the characteristics of each are quite distinct.

The upper cavern, which the EXAMINER party followed for five miles, is a division in itself. The main cave divides just a short way from the entrance, and while one has a general upward trend, the other descends.

From each of these main caverns, innumerable corridors branch out above, below and to each side. Some of these are larger than the main cavern. They follow no general direction, but twist and intersect and divide and redivide and, in many cases lead back to the original passage.

One day, the EXAMINER party, after steadily plodding forward for six hours, found itself back almost at the entrance to the cave.

In the upper fork of the main corridor is the channel of the creek [River Styx] which flows from the mouth of the cave. You cannot see the water all the time, but it generally follows the line of the corridor. In some places there has formed over it a thick layer of stalactite stone, and the water runs beneath it like a river under the ice.

The lowest corridor could not be followed a great distance because the columns have filled some of the narrow passages. But these can be opened to allow passage.

The Hot Room

From the cave that begins high up on the bluff there are a great many lateral passages. It was in one of these that one of the early visitors claims to have found a room so hot that he could only remain in it a few seconds. The heat, he claimed, came from an opening in the floor of the room. The chamber was full of steam. He described his route as being past the Ghost's Hall, and beyond a series of enormous vaulted chambers. He only reached the hot room once. He failed to mark his way and could not find it again. The EXAMINER party searched for this strange place. Although the Ghost's Hall and big vaulted rooms were found without much trouble, there was no discovery of a steam pit. That is hardly remarkable as nearly every room had half-a-dozen exits and these sub-divide almost every few feet.

It was impossible to map this complexity during the brief but excitement-packed EXAMINER'S exploration.

```
Phantom Hunters' Valhalla

    The Ghost Hall is a room per-
haps sixty feet long. At the end of it
the ceiling and walls are nearly
together. On first entering the
room, nothing is to be seen. The
far end of the cave appears simply
black but as the light from the
torches crept into the niches, first
one shrouded figure and then
another loomed up in the dark
alcove. It was grisly enough for a
minute to suit the most exacting
hunter of phantoms.
```

Their Geological Formation

Professor Henry G. Hanks, California State Mineralogist, speaking of the discovery on July 11, said that the Oregon caves were interesting and remarkable and doubtless soon will become a popular resort for tourists.

"In a general way," he said, "they differ but little from the other caves in the State." But from their description given to the cave in the EXAMINER, they are more beautiful in formation and much larger.

The caves in San Luis Obispo County, the Bass Cave in Shasta County, the one near the town of Volcano in Amador County, and the Caves of the Catacombs and Crystal Cave in Calaveras County, all have the same general style and are produced in a precisely similar way as these great caves in Oregon. But when the California caves' size is compared with the dimensions of these newly explored caverns in Oregon, they sink into insignificance.

There is a charm about these openings in the earth to the human mind that is quite unaccountable. Most people delight in exploring a natural cave. The experience is a pleasure mixed with a certain amount of dread, as they penetrate deeper into the earth and see for the first time gloomy caverns artificially lighted by the lamps they carry.

Limestone Cave Formation

The geological formation is the same as in the caves found in all limestone countries. In my report to the Government on the known caves in the United States in 1886, I explained the way in which these caves were formed. Carbonate of lime is soluble to a slight degree in pure cold water and more so when carbonic acid is present. Water in a limestone country is generally in this condition. In percolating through a calcareous formation – a formation of the nature of limestone – water bears away a notable portion of the rock in solution which continued through a geological period of long duration, manifests itself in cavernous openings generally known as caves.

—Prof. Henry G. Hanks
California State Mineralogist (1891)

Little Drops of Water

The way in which the numerous stalactites and stalagmites are formed makes an interesting study. The stalactites hang like stony icicles from the roof of a cave while stalagmites rise from the floor immediately beneath them. Little drops of water constantly dripping, but at long intervals from some point in the roof, gradually form a small hanging protrusion of stone which in long centuries form into a perfect hanging pillar of stone.

By the same process, the constant dripping of water to the floor builds the stalagmite. As the ages roll by, the two become united and form a perfect pillar of stone whose sides are slowly but surely being added to by the water as it finds its way down and leaves its mineral deposits.

Stalactites hang from ceiling as stalagmites reach for them from the floor. "Simply amazing; nothing short of astounding" declared Professor John LaCoste, Whitworth College, to author in spring 1965.

By the same process, the constant dripping of water to the floor builds the stalagmite. As the ages roll by, the two become united and form a perfect pillar of stone whose sides are slowly but surely being added to by the water as it finds its way down and leaves its mineral deposits.

It is curious to consider that these excavations have been made by the slow, solvent action of water falling drop by drop, and that the same process is going on today but the growing of the forms is imperceptible to the senses. Some faint idea may also be gained of the great age of these limestone rocks by considering these factors.

The drops do not form rapidly. The tip of the stalactite must be watched for some time before the fall will be seen to occur and considerable time passes before another drop of water takes its place. This slow operation has been going on for centuries. ◇

The "Examiner's" Expedition's Further. Discoveries in the Great Cave in Southern Oregon.

What an "Examiner" Party Now at Work in the Cave Has. Brought Under the Torchlight—How New Passages Were Broken Into by Hammer and Drill and a Way Made Where No Man's Foot Had Ever Trodden Before--Down Into a Well That Led to a Stream Coursing Its Way Beneath the Mountain—A Strange Underground Cataract and Stranger Formations of Rock.

CAVE STATION (Or.), May 26.—Down in the underland, down in the wonderland, into the world made by ~~~~ who cleaved ~~~~

This major feature article was written by F. B. Millard, a reporter for the San Francisco Examiner. (It is cited in the bibliography.) Some of the microfilm is unclear therefore our account allows some license for clarity. Readers are reminded that some of the chambers identified in the article now have different names and may not be on the present tour route. —Editor

~~~~ phrase is that ~~~~ cession and interminable tangle of corridors, crawling ways and chambers known as the Great Oregon Cave. The story of the discovery of the cavern and of its first intelligent exploration was

PART I

HEADLINE:

The "EXAMINER'S" Expedition's Further Discoveries in the Great Cave in Southern Oregon.

What an "EXAMINER" Party Now at Work in the Cave Has Brought Under the Torchlight – How New Passages Were Broken Into by Hammer and Drill and a Way Made Where No Man's Foot Had Ever Trodden Before – Down Into a Well That Led to a Stream Coursing Its Way Beneath the Mountain – A Strange Underground Cataract and Stranger Formations of Rock.

CAVE STATION (Or.), May 26, [1894] — Down in the underland, down in the wonderland, into the world made by sightless Titans, who cleaved and hewed, smote and sweated – an abysmal world of blackness and yet of beauty, a world of unsounded depths and unmeasured breadth, a world with the sun shut out!

Such a lame phrase is that wonderful succession and interminable tangle of corridors, crawling ways and chambers known as the Great Oregon Cave. The story of the discovery of the cavern and of its first intelligent exploration was told in the EXAMINER by Mr. Charles Michelson three years ago. Since that time, many persons have burnt coal oil and candles in its dark recesses, and a few have penetrated the corridors so far as to open new "rooms," as they are called, and behold crystalline wonders never gazed upon before. And yet there remained other places where light had never entered. It was to view these and give account thereof that the EXAMINER sent out our party a fortnight ago.

Supplied with provisions to last for months, if need be, and equipped with cameras, large and small, torches, candles, lanterns, twine, rubber boots and clothing and magnesium powder enough to flash-light the Inferno itself, we left Grants Pass in Southern Oregon, to go over the wagon road and trail to the cave. After a pleasant journey through timber land that breathed of fire balsam and azaleas, we reached the log cabin at Cave Station where we rested for the night. Before a big log fire, in one of the cabins, Nickerson, the cave guide, told tales of wonderful things in the great cavern nearby in the mountain, and Uncle Jack Henderson, whose Rembrandt face looked strong and characterful in the firelight, went over the story of the finding of the cave. Outside, the smoke drift from the stump fires hung along the mountain's scalp and a brook below the cabin talked to us as its waters crashed over rocks.

The sky was partially obscured by puffy clouds but there was a glory of stars twinkling to us as we went into the cabin and climbed into our blankets. The night was cold. There was no wind. The next morning there was a foot of snow on the ground and the fir branches were heavy with it. After an early breakfast, we trudged up the cave trail, over a rustic bridge that crossed a noisy stream, and onward to the upper or main entrance of the cave. Here a few of the timid ones looked about for what they feared might be a last view of the sun, but nothing was in their view except snow. Blacker than black Hades yawned the mouth of that cave in its setting of white, but the gloom faded away before the torch and lantern. There was a chill of the draught near the entrance only – it was gone when we turned the first angle. It was down a ladder, over a rocky floor and down another ladder. Thus far we had walked erect. Then came a series of places where the roof of the narrow corridor came down in a way to affront one, and then it was hands and knees.

Past Old Nick's Bedchamber, whose invitation – a short ladder – we did not heed just then, for we were going straight on to the Ghost Chamber, the great central cavern, and past the Eagle Room and the Bridal Chamber we made our way, at what pace we might, for it was both good or bad going.

The main silvery formation of limestone and the gritty sort, too, had been left behind, and the region of calcareous pendants and deposits had been reached. Gray stalactites and some alabaster whiteness and of a length that astonished one unaccustomed to the affairs of small caverns, impended from the corridor and from that of the "rooms" along the way and from the shelves seen everywhere in the great cave.

What seemed to be the end of the corridor sprang into view but there was always a way onward, even though it demanded what we came to designate as "belly work," sliding along on the stomach, propelled by fingers and toes. This kind of going was infrequent and there were only four crawls, the longest some twenty feet on the way to the Ghost Chamber.

Giant powder has done its work well since an earlier trip and there is now no more crawling from the main entrance to the great room where the white spirits of the cavern hold their revels.

None of the ladders are long and they are all strongly built and easy to climb or descend, and now that the crawls are gone, one can make his or her way to the Ghost Chamber with comparative ease and perfect safety. Of course it is not like walking down a paved street as a matter of fact, though it is preferable to some horse trails one finds in the mountains with four Oregon miles ahead of you and the night coming on.

It was up an Aladdin's pathway of gray limestone, fringed and overhung with tallowy stalactites, over a backboard on each side of which glittered beds of pure lime crystals, down a short ladder, over a floor of frozen milk, into a room that dazzled you with its brilliant crustations from pipestem points and burr-like crystalline balls, with millions of needles on a background of elephant-hide and mouse-color, and then on to a nameless room which we dubbed the "Howdah," because of the resemblance its chief ornament had to the thing they shoot Royal Bengal Tigers from in the school geographics.

A seemingly plastic mass that flowed form the side of the roof fingered out into giant stalactites and bat-winged shapes that showed high ridges and imaginary forms. Anything you wanted to believe you were seeing was here. Do you want to see a shapely urn? There it was. But one side seemed a little warped but that didn't matter. Did you want an old sedan chair, a cradle or a throne? There they were. As for animate objects, the place was fairly alive with them. Each member of the party made out something to suit his fancy and which once he pointed it out to the others, they saw it and would have sworn to the resemblance. There were goddesses of liberty, peasant girls, sailors and soldiers. When, however, the artist of the party pointed out a Keith landscape with a gnarled oak in foreground, and a man in a red shirt and cowboy hat in the middle distance, is was as though time had moved on.

And so the party passed though room after room. Rooms with high ceilings and plenty of stalactites, rooms with low ceilings and no stalactites at all. Rooms with high sounding names such as the King's hallway and the Princes' Boudoir, and impish names such as the Devil's Kitchen and the Brownies Bathroom. There were anonymous rooms as interesting as any of them, and all opening upon and around corridors that lead on and on, only God knows where. We stuck to the main passage. It was a queer caravan that made its uncertain and tortuous way along the mazy path toward the Ghost Chamber. Our Guide, Nickerson, led off with his smoky torch that showed up well enough when he was straight ahead, but which left us in total darkness when he turned two angles and left me with another smoky torch following a blind lead that might or might not bring his light into view at the next turn. Our artist trailed a big black portfolio, to which he clung closer than to the ladders he descended, and photographers Tibbitts and Jensen pushed and hauled a big camera case that rumbled over the rocky floor and broke off a stalagmite here and there.

John O. Quinn, wearing a [hat] ___ Backas, Colonel L. D. Stone, J. L. Gittings and R. B. Elder followed along; each bearing a torch. The last five named gentlemen, who had come up to the cave from San Francisco with the EXAMINER party, took a great interest in all this work and remained with us during the greater part of the first day's exploration.

Just before the ante-chamber of the Ghost Room the guide pointed out a dark hollow which, from its shape and exterior view, took the name of the Tomb of Rameses the Third, applied by classical Mr. Quinn. Near by was what the guide was pleased

THE DAZZLING INTERIOR OF MONTE CRISTO'S TREASURE CH
[Sketched by an "Examiner" artist.]

The dazzling interior of Monte Cristo's Treasure Chamber.
[Sketched by an "Examiner" artist.]

to term the statue of George Washington. In a rough way the object did take on the lines of a statue, but why George Washington any more than anyone else nobody could tell.

We ascended some rough steps and stood in the ante-room. Unlike the other rooms spoken of along the way, there is a good deal in this ante-room of which nothing has been written. In the first place, there are the pillars at the right of the entrance and nearly at the end of the chamber standing solemn and solidly against an inky background. They are about five inches thick

53

and eight feet high, and there are three of them. At their foot is a basin of pure water, lined with crystals. It is cold to almost freezing, this water, utterly devoid of vegetation or animal matter is quickly sought by the perspiring cave travelers. The stalagmites, aside from those that joined the stalactites to make the white columns near the end of the room, are quite small here and are flattened out more than in some of the other chambers, but the low stalactites are long and beautiful. Here, as elsewhere in the cave, one looks in vain for that transparency suggested by the many drippings from ceiling and heapings up on floor; but when one stops to think that all this lime formation is opaque, one looks no longer for the impossible. The nearest that transparency is reached is toward the ends if those wonderful pipestems made by low dripping of water through new-forming stalactites that grow straight down on all sides, making long pencil-shaped pendants instead of cones. Breaking these off, one finds them hollow,* and they may be used as pipestems, and are so used by some of the ____.

The ante-room is imposing. Its walls are high, though they vary considerably in height, and the floor is broad though rough. There are great scout-outs and convexities with here and there a neat little pitfall that demands close attention on penalty of a fall or sprain. Starting at the back of the room near the pillars, you face the doorway to the Ghost Chamber, on which nearly everything of anticipation regarding the cave is sure to center.

> **We pass the grim portal in mute procession and stood in a great blackness that our torches refused to dissipate. It was the blackness of the Ghost Chamber, into which we had passed after nearly two hours of hard underground travel, having traversed a distance which our guide assured us was not less than three miles, but about which we all had our doubts, some thinking they had gone farther and others not so far. But there we were and the underworld lay all before us, fresh and untrodden, for the previous explorations had been nearly all just to the great central room and we were going beyond it.**

---

* The reference here is obviously to what are called "soda straws." Refer to Glossary.
—Editor

Very few passages leading away from the Ghost Chamber had been followed and these for a short distance only. In fact, our guide, who knew more about the cave than any one, confessed his inability to conduct us more than a short distance beyond the place where we stood. It was necessary then, that we should take a good look about us, and so we scattered about the Ghost Chamber looking for places of egress. It was then that we took in the immensity of the great hall, though this seemed more by feeling and inspiration than by actual sight, for a torch is but a feeble thing in that heavy underground darkness that weighs upon one and tires one as no other darkness can. In a little cavern, with the walls close to you at every turn., the light of a lantern or a candle suffices to drive away the gloom, but not so in the capital Ghost Chamber.

The whole room seems to be built up of soapy limestone, the brittle sort that is found at the surface, and for the most part it was dry, only a little water trickling down in the east corner near the great masses of white, looking for all the world like sheets of melted tallow that hang from the wall there, making the only part of the room that reflects any light from lantern or torch. For the rest the walls are all of a grimy brown, and have sharp angles of rock, jutting out in what seem impossible ways. There are vagrant rocks there with no visible means of support, and rocks as evenly balanced as the minds of great statesmen. Some of these stony monsters look as if a hand set upon them would hurl them down into the abysm of unknown depth that looks so innocent and shallow there in the even darkness that hides them all.

From a central view the points of light that came from torch and lantern seemed near enough at hand, but when you came to grope your way over the rough floor toward one of them, you found they were not so close after all.

We went with the guide to view the pool in the north passage, near the big cavern. It is a small pond of limpid water, three to four feet deep in the low corridor that crooks a short elbow and leads back into the Ghost Room again. Here in the pool was where the gummed boots came in handily, for passage along this corridor is hardly possible without wading, as the banks of the pool are very narrow and give one a slim and slippery foothold.

There are a great many passages that lead out of the Ghost Room and the EXAMINER party, with its guide – five men in all – followed, leaving the other gentlemen in the Ghost Room where another guide joined them and soon afterward showed them the way out. Nearly all the passages explored were short. They would make a few twists and turns and then lead back into the Ghost Room.

> Sometimes a corridor, beginning at the main hall, would loop over or under itself two or three times in a most confusing way and would re-enter the big room within 50 feet of the place where we started. This shows that the whole region in the neighborhood of the Ghost Room is one great honeycomb, or perhaps a better simile would be the teredo eaten pile.

But for beauty, the passages lacked not at all. Along some of them were little rooms, say 10 by 20 feet and even smaller, each with its individual charm whether of crystals of cones or what the guide called "gingerhead ornaments, scallops and curly-cuoe." [*sic.*]   And there, as well as everywhere else in the great

Musical Stalactites —!

> And the musical stalactites. It is hardly to be credited how true their tone and how nearly they ran the gamut. We found a chamber we called The Cathedral because of the beautiful, bell-like notes that could be struck upon its long stalactites. There were the eight true notes of the scale and some to spare for "accidentals" and chords. On these we played "Coronation," "Sweet Bye-and-Bye," and "Home Sweet Home." Although the playing was halting and imperfect, being *adagio* where it should have been *allegretto*, and *fortissimo* where the *pianissimo* should have come in, the tones were loud and clear. They were cheering, too, to those of us who felt the oppression of the darkness and the chilliness that would assert itself in spite of much exertion.

cave, were those strange scribblings of nature, those strange pencillings of nature learning how to sketch. Many of these were meaningless scrawls, but here you saw the almost perfect eagle, and there the all but finished statue of a nymph whose hair fell below her waist, and whose face shown in the torchlight.

At last we hit upon a passage that led straight away. We hiked for over half-an-hour, and we were rid of what one of our party called "that perpetually bobbing-up Ghost Room."

The way led downward at first and along a muddy bottom, where it was easy to scratch our arrows [on the walls] that pointed the way back out of the maze of cross-channels and intersecting corridors.

Soon the arrows were scratched upon what seemed to be granite, but which was not granite, for the imitation limestone mimics every kind of mineral formation from white sandstone to the blackest and glossiest of gold. The way led upward, through V-shaped crevices in the rocks and under masses that had fallen from the ceiling leaving just crawling space and not more, and then room to walk erect and make good time. We went creeping along a backbone then suddenly came upon the end of the passage. The stalactites forming thickly there made a sign of "No Thoroughfare," and out came the hammers. It was 20 minutes work to spoil one of the prettiest of mineral cataracts and make a passage under the end of broken stalactites and on to where there was walking space. The squeeze was a tight one, and not a few of the smaller pendant candles and pipestems ["soda straws"] were cracked off by our heads, while ugly pencil-points from the floor nearly jabbed out our eyes. A knock of the head against a good solid stalactite – the kind that does not give way – was a frequent experience in all the places where we broke our way through, as we had to do many times that day.

Coming to a place where there were two very promising intersecting channels, one joining the other over a shelf, below which the first proceeded, we were at a loss to know which road to take. We rested in the high-roofed chamber which formed this junction place, sitting down on the cold, white stones.

The finest intaglios had here been cut by nature. Frosted work by curious design, delicate tracery in patterns not known of many encrustation's, and crystals whose points caught the torchlight and sent it back as rays from those bits of carbon insignificantly paltry in comparison, which women wear in their ears. Through this chamber and along the downward course we went, leaving the unexplored passage that led over the shelf and away into the darkness. (We might try this later.) Wilder and wilder grew the scene. Doré would have gloated over it for his "Inferno" composition.*

Great fingers, hands and arms of black rock were held out to hold us back. They were not of stalactite formation. But of that grainless rock that seems like cast iron. On anyone of the fingers of hands, large or small, I would trust my life implicitly, after the tests we gave that formation. We descended on rough ladders of rock never touched by human feet before and kept going down these and along gentler slopes until we came to a barrier. Jag-tooth jaws of rock closed down tightly right in front of us right on the floor. They were like a grating over a well, and to get into that well the hammers and a short drill had to be used.

As we hammered on the teeth and pieces of rock fell down the hole it seemed to take a good deal of time for [the pieces] to reach the bottom. They would go ringing from one little projection to another and then we would hear a splash. There was water down there. How much of it we could not tell. Here might be the end of the passage, and we were only an hour-and-a-half from the Ghost Chamber – not such a great distance after all.

> The compass told us that we were going east which was deeper under the mountain, but the compass may have lied, for the mountain has iron and the needle twitches sometimes, and sometimes the needle will point in any direction it is set.

Nickerson made the chips of rock fly, and he worked so hard that when he had a hole large enough to admit a passage, he was too tired to go down into the hole.

I swung a lantern down through the opening. It banged against the rocks and stuck, so that I could not see the bottom, but on putting my ear close down to the hole, I could hear the rushing of a stream. What light the lantern afforded showed that

---

*Gustave Doré, (1832-1883) illustrator, whose bizarre fantasy created vast dreamlike scenes as when, in 1861, he illustrated Dante's *Inferno*.

LETTING THE "EXAMINER" CORRESPONDENT
DOWN INTO VERNE'S WELL.
[*From a sketch by the "Examiner" artist.*]

BREAKING A PASSAGE THROUGH THE STALACTITES ON THE WAY TO
VERNE'S WELL AND THE CATARACT.
[From a sketch by the "Examiner" artist.]

the hole pitched down straight for about 30 feet and then slanted off into unknown depths.

Attaching the end of a 200-foot rope to my body, and taking a tight grip upon it, I swung off thorough the hole, the rope being paid out slowly by two men above. I had let the lantern stay where it had lodged, so that there was a little light, but I missed my torch not being able to carry it, as I had to keep my hands free. I felt a scaly foothold here and there, little more than a toehold, I might say, but I trusted none of them, letting the rope bear all my weight, until I reached the little shelf where the lantern was stuck. I disengaged the lantern rope which had become entangled in the scraggy rocks, and let the lantern swing free into the chasm, which widened toward the bottom. I could hear the rush of the water more plainly, but I could not see the water yet. It was rather a ticklish position to be in, but I called out for the men above to let out more rope and swung off the little shelf. They let the rope out with a jerk that made me loose my breath for a moment and the noose under my arms slipped so

60

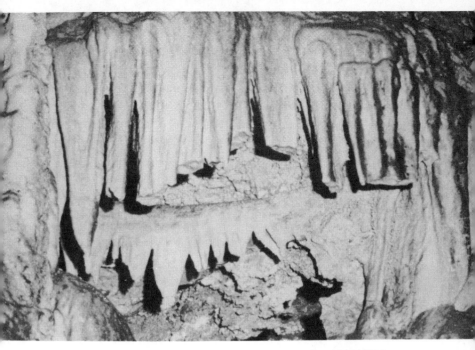

Broken stalactites. Cave location not identified. This photograph loosely resembles the artist's sketch on opposite page. Breaking any formation in the Oregon Caves National Monument today is a punishable offense.

tightly that I felt like a cinched up pony. Then they let me down more easily and I was soon on a shelf that was only a foot or two above the water. I could see then that the water would not come over my rubber boots, and so I waded across the stream to a gravely bank. I had to sit and rest on a rock for a little while. I called this hole Jules Verne's Well.

I lighted a candle that I had in my pocket and leaving the lantern as a sort of guide for the way back I went on along the subterranean stream, sometimes wading in the water and sometimes walking or crawling on the bank.

It was a good wide passage down there, and for the most part high enough to walk erect. The formation was much looser than above. It was chiefly of dripping rocks that looked just ready to fall. On the sides there was a good deal of silt, that would become limestone in a thousand years or so, but which was anything but firm just then. The water had cut into it and it was crumbling down here and there in a way I did not fancy.

I had made several turns and the light of the lantern was wholly cut off, when I heard a rock fall behind me. I looked up and saw what were probably just such other rocks imbedded in the silt above my head. I dodged past one of these, and my candle sputtered out in the water [that was] trickling down from above.

The darkness of a heavily curtained bedroom on a moonless night or the darkness of a photographers darkroom with the dull red light gone out, was as nothing compared with the utter blackness of that deeply hidden waterway under the mountain.

To me it was about four hours before I could get my candle lighted, though to the grinning imps who saw me wildly striking matches on wet rocks, it was perhaps not more than two minutes. Finally, going a few steps farther and making another turn, I heard the roar of a waterfall. I looked at my watch. It was late and there was that hard climb back of me, so I put off going to the falls until next day.

Going up that rope was a good deal harder than coming down, but they hauled me out of the depths at last. What an eerie experience this had been. I had carefully explored where no other human had ever explored or even walked before.

On the following day I went down into the same hole again, Colonel Stone going with me, and we two soon reached the underground cataract which we named Stone's Falls. At the side of the falls was a great mass of limestone standing almost perpendicularly. It was cold, black, and wet. Here was the only way that led on and the mass was 20 feet high. Standing on Colonel Stone's shoulders, I managed to reach a place where I could get a foothold on the slippery rock and scrambled up to what seemed like a small passage above, on a shelf. But it was only a pocket. Stone's Falls proved to be the end of the cave.

The water poured down from a huge spout through which nothing could pass upward. Down stream the wall closed in up-on the water a short distance from the hole that afforded in-gress to the waterway. This is the hole I had decided to call Jules Verne's Well, with hazy reference to the great natural shaft of which the wild Frenchman wrote in "Mysterious Island."

But although this way on has closed down in front of us, there are corridors and corridors – even more corridors and we are still at work in them. ◇

PART II
1894 EXAMINER'S Expedition
(Original headline missing)

Cave Station (Or.) May 27. — Blasting and cutting in the crawl ways of the great Oregon cave continued during the whole stay there of the EXAMINER party. The work was done under the direction of the party, as well as was the work of exploration. The use of giant powder in the low corridors on the way to the Ghost Chamber, as the main cavern is called, was with no immediate view of facilitating the work of the explorers who did not wish to waste valuable time in slow traveling over places where other people had been before, and there was the further desire to make the way easier for future visitors. It was not many days before the time of passage from the upper entrance of the cave to the Ghost Chamber was reduced to thirty minutes. If you want to rush and sweat you can make it in a few minutes less, but the slow travel is safe travel in the great cave, for there are ladders and more ladders, and you would better leave the fast ladder-climbing to the city firemen who know how to do it.

Coal oil, bacon and beans, apple sauce, bread and butter, and miles and miles of twine were kept in the Ghost Chamber for our daily use and consumption. It was noted that the cool air of the cavern preserved the eatables in a remarkable way. The cave is better than a refrigerator for preserving meats, as was demonstrated when some fresh beef was left in it for several days. It has this advantage too, over a refrigerator that a freezing temperature is not required. There is always a strong draught of pure cold air sucking through the cavern. It is not so noticeable in the larger chambers, but in the smaller ones and in the crawling spaces, it is generally felt with a vengeance.

> **Many times when I was crawling along a low, narrow passage the wind would keep my torch flaring like mad, and of a sudden it would go out, leaving me in total darkness and unable for a time to light a match because of the strength of the breeze.**

For the next few days after going down into Verne's Well to Stone's Falls, we continued to explore the cave in the neighborhood of the Ghost Chamber, but while we found many rooms that were interesting from a geological standpoint, we did not find any that were large enough and beautiful enough to compare with the best of those already discovered.

It was on the sixth day after our arrival that we made the discovery that was to be of great importance to us and to those who would come after us into the great cavern. This was the finding of Monte Cristo's Treasure Chamber.

It will be recalled that earlier, in the lower cavern where we found Verne's Well, there was an intersecting passage that led from the Verne corridor over a shelf. Something kept nagging at me that I should make time to get back to explore that shelf. On going back to this shelf we found that the upper passage was open for several feet beyond, but that it soon "closed down," to use the phrase we adopted with respect to many of the corridors.

Stalactites hung down in great arms three to four feet long, and stalagmites beneath them rose to points that nearly met the upper pendants, and in some cases did actually meet and form pillars or columns. These calerous barriers were very beautiful, but they were barriers none the less, and though we were loath to destroy them, it was absolutely necessary to do so in order to advance.

It was an hour's work to break off enough of the mineral icicles and roof-pointing fingers to admit us on our onward passage, and even when we were ready to start we found that the way was rough enough to suit even the most adventurous spelunker.

I do not know nor am I able to conceive of any harder going than that through a mass of stalactites and stalagmites that bar your way even though it be partly cleared by the hammer and drill.

> You are reminded at least once a minute that you have a head, and one's head is a good deal softer than any stalactite ever grown. Where the way seems to be the clearest, your head will sometimes go "ka-thump" against a flinty pendant that will resound in your body all the way down to your heels from the knock. And as there is no help for you, swearing often comes easily.*

We had a great lot of rough going but the way led upward. That was a great encouragement. It is strange how reluctantly and carefully a party of cave explorers will pick their way downward over a comparative easy road, when if that road led upward they would go along with perfect cheerfulness. There are several reasons for this aside from the "excelsior" idea, and one of these is that more water is encountered on the downward slopes and the formation is generally darker.

There was a good deal of climbing over narrow chasms that sounded deep when a stone was tossed down into them, but the

---

* Hard hats are strongly recommended for cave visitors even to the present time for there are many "low bridges" under which spelunkers will pass. No party of visitors, including the hard-hatted guides, is known to pass through these caves without someone's head being bashed by a ceiling rock. Hard hats can be rented inexpensively at the ticket counter. —Editor

stalactites always made the best of handles for a good hard grip, and as long as one had hold of a stalagmite twice as big as his thumb there was no danger of anyone having to collect his life insurance in a hurry. We entered a sort of hallway where there was a large shelf on the right, and what seemed great masses of what seemed tallow dripping running from it like a frozen waterfall. The formation was about the color of tallow, too, and took on all sorts of shapes. There was what one of our party who named a scene Solomon's Bedstead. It generally resembled a bedstead, too, and was very neatly spread with a ghostly white coverlet, but the mattress certainly did not appear to be soft enough to be inviting, even to we weary cave explorers. Above the bed was a sort of canopy and from this tricked a little water, which added to the discomforts of the bed, and confirmed our belief that it was not as good a place to sleep as one might find in the What Cheer House.

There were no ladders to go down, but the ropes came in very handily at particularly ugly jumping-off places. It seemed strange that in a channel that nearly always led upward there should be those great sink holes. They could be accounted for only by the action of water in former ages. This theory seemed the most plausible when the mud that lay at the bottom of nearly every one of them was taken into account.

We made the most irregular procession along there. One man would lead the way and be away up above everybody else. The next man would probably be crawling on his stomach ten feet from the first man's heels. Another would be down in a sink hole and the fourth sliding down a rope away in the rear. We were in just such a position when the man ahead yelled out: "This is the end of it. It closes down here." We were tired and disgusted so we stopped in our tracks and sat down to rest.

"What's that opening over there"? I asked, pointing to the left, where I noted a black blotch. When there is no reflection of our torchlight from a wall, just a black blotch means no wall – a hole in the wall. An entrance maybe? Nobody knew. Nobody had looked into it.

One of the men stuck a torch through an opening in the stalactites and called out "Big Chamber." He went on. We followed

ON THE WAY TO VERNE'S WELL AND THE CATARACT—A HARD CRAWL
[From a sketch by the "Examiner" artist.]

On the way to Verne's Well and the cataract—a hard crawl.
[From a sketch by the "Examiner" artist.]

at his heels. "This looks like it – finest room yet," said Nickerson the guide.

There were pillars along the way. They stood pure white and straight as arrows. There were stalactites yards long and great clumps of stalagmites that cluttered the floor and made the passage like one through a forest where small trees had been cut off high up from the ground. A little way ahead it looked as if we were at the end, but the hammers were wielded vigorously, and the crackle of falling stalactites sounded through the chamber. The passage was made.

The Crystal Palace

We crawled upward into a room that fairly dazzled us by its brilliancy as we held our torches high. Crystals. There were crystals everywhere. The whole floor was ablaze with them.

They shown from little shelves along the wall and they sparkled from what seemed like caskets set in the roof. They descended from long pipestems and pencils; sometimes in clusters and sometimes singly. What a glorious sight to behold. We realized that no man had ever viewed this amazing spectacle before. This was a fairyland of crystals.

"Keep off the Grass"! was the cry with which we greeted a thoughtless member of the party who would have wandered through this wonderful hall with his muddy boots. The crystals crackled under his feet and he sprang to the rock on which we were standing.

Before a shelf that was radiant with millions of needlepoints

68

of the crystals lay a pool of water. It was so clear and pure and so bedded by the beautiful crystalline formation that we did not observe at first that it was water. On another shelf a little to the right was a large white chest, with an irregularly formed lid, and somehow this helped in naming the room of crystals. We dubbed it "Monte Cristo's Treasure Chamber."

The party filed out and I paused to pick up a few specimens. They were pure white but would probably turn to yellow after a few days of sunlight, but it would remain white for ages in that deep underground room. The sound of the footprints of the other men died away.

> In here, in this fairyland of crystals, there was a silence so perfect that I found myself straining my ear to catch some faintest sound. There was none.

It was simply awful to stay in there alone. The white sprays of crystal stood out upon such perfect inner blackness, the shadows beyond were so pal-pable as to seem like living presences. You could reach forth and touch them. They were as solid as anything else, in that chamber of riches that to a lost explorer would soon become a chamber of the weirdest horrors.

I ran out and along the passage and joined my friends. It is not so bad to be alone in the dark there when you have something to do, but to sit down in silence and let the darkness weigh upon you, as it is bound to do whenever you cease all motions, is unbearable. The darkest dungeon in San Quentin would seem cheerful in comparison.

There were some tall openings leading off from the passage into the treasure chamber, but there was no way through the chamber onward. It was with great difficulty that we opened a way for a short distance on one of these branch-offs, but when it closed down to a hole not much too large for a rat to fill with comfort we gave it up and left off work for the day.

With a young mountaineer named Frank Frakes, and with the guide Nickerson, whose knowledge of the cave had by this time been thoroughly shown to us, I went off into the Bell Chamber and on to the Organ Loft, places already well known to the cave visitors, and tried to find a way on toward the south, the

"When the photographers flashed their magnesium light upon the end of the cavern and the whole wall over there stood out in ragged relief, the instant darkness that followed the blinding flash was thicker than ever." —F. B. Millard, The San Francisco *Examiner* 1894

general direction taken by the main passage from the entrance near Cave Station.

With the greatest care, we searched all about for some way that might lead on from the neighborhood of the Bell Chamber, but for a time we were disappointed. It was Frakes' good luck to find a hole that seemed to be the right way on, and in spite of Nickerson's belief that no passage existed there, the young mountain boy was soon quite away in advance, crawling down among the rocks that lay strewn all about in a most chaotic way. It seemed as though the rocks had fallen from the roof of a large cave that had existed in there at some past time.

Frakes called out to us, and we followed along over the toughest going for any great distance that can well be found in the main cavern. But somebody had been there before us. We saw the initials of J. C. Kincaid an Oregonian who had dated the rocks in many places with huge numerals "92's." We would have sworn that the marks were not more than a few days old at the furthest, and they looked to be about 5 minutes old in some places. Kincaid's figures were traced in the mud here and there and even in this formation they stood out clearly and as fresh as though but made the day before. I had noted the same peculiarity in other parts of the cavern, the strangest thing being a name traced with a pencil on a stalactite in 1878, which had held the lead [sic.] since that time without losing a particle of its substance.

Kincaid had made arrows pointing backward toward the entrance, but we stretched a string along and thus made assurance doubly sure as to our safe return. Soon the markings ceased. Kincaid had gone no further, as his lights had nearly given out, a fact which I learned later.

The formation was dark, and there were no stalactites. There was plenty of room at times to walk upright, but a great deal of the way was over large rocks, along which we crawled into rooms hardly large enough to swing a cat in. Finally we emerged into a large cavern. It was about 30 x 80 feet in floor area 10 to 20 feet high. It was chaos itself in there, the rocks pointing in great scraggly masses in every direction from sides, floor an ceiling. Blacker than the "Black Hole of Calcutta." And wilder than any of the other large chambers of the great cavern, the Bogie Room, as we called it, is a feature of the cave that visitors will not search for with such great enthusiasm as they will for the beautiful crystal rooms two hours nearer the entrance.

The next day we explored in vain the side walls of the Bogie Room and the way leading into it for a passage that should still lead onward. We did not find any that day, nor the next. Finally, photographer Jensen, a young man named Zeverly and myself made the search such a thorough one as to give us the key. Through a most dismal crawling way the opening led on to an Inferno that rivaled the region at Verne's Well. Here we made a discovery. It was the complete skeletons of two large bears. The Lord only knows how they made their way in here and how long they had been there. We removed a few perfect bones and one or two large teeth, but nearly all of the other bones crumbled on touching them – the action of the damp and the insidious lime making them soft as cheese.

We called this place the "Ursine Catacombs." It was frightfully damp in there, the water spraying down from a well so deep that looking up from its bottom we could not see the top, though it may not have been more than 75 feet over us. Our theory was that the bears had fallen down from some high place into the cave, but where the opening was we could not discover.

As there were masses of rock all around that have evidentialy been displaced at no long time back it seemed that the opening had been covered by the earth or rocks caving into it.

In the succeeding days we made no great discoveries, although we opened several little passages into small rooms. I believe that here, as in the Mammoth Cave of Kentucky, it will be many years before the end of all the tangled passages shall be reached. A little dynamite and a good deal of drilling and picking may open new caverns in the mountain there greater than any yet been found.

It is the purpose of the company owning the cave to light it with electricity. A large hotel is to be built at Cave Station, and under superintendent A. B. Smith, the work of developing the cave is to go on until its extent shall be known with greater definiteness than at present. ◇ —Written in 1894

Early-day visitors to the Oregon caves.
Scene is in Joaquim Miller Chapel. Note candle-lanterns made from tin cans and fellow sitting on floor leaning against Grand Column and another leaning on the column. Today everyone is asked to adopt a "hands off" policy for cave preservation.

The Mammoth Colum
Oregon Caves
'23 Patterson

Guide Dick Rowley at Grand Column, called "Mammoth Column" by photographer Patterson in 1923.

Chapter 3

Joaquin Miller on Oregon's Marble Halls
or
Lost in the Caves Twice in the Same Day

> **In true spelunker's language, one is never "lost" in a cave, merely "temporarily disoriented."**

Under the border between Oregon and California lie some wonderful caverns in a marble mountain practically unknown to a world that will some day list them among its chief wonders. Stories of these marble grottoes, five levels of glittering chambers with a basement apparently bottomless, have filtered out of Oregon forests during the last thirty years from hunters who have found their way up the difficult trails to the mysterious little doorway in the marble cliff.

These stories fired the zeal of Joaquin Miller [1839-1913], famous prospector after the hidden treasures of the earth and *poet laureate* of the western mountains.

Here follows his account of his recent trip to these unknown marvels, one of the first descriptions of a place that will have its own literature when it shall have been made accessible to the world.

—Remarks of Charles Sedgwick Aiken, for *Sunset Magazine* September 1909
—Edited for this book by Bert Webber

Poet Joaquin Miller wrote that the wondrous marble halls of Oregon lie close against the northern line (42° N. Lat.) of California and it is not unreasonable to believe it may be found finally that they pierce entirely through the marble summits of the Siskiyou Mountains and have an opening on the California side. The cave was only partially explored but he assured his readers that these halls were not newly discovered by any means. In that era they were accessible only during the summer months and even then by a route that was almost impassable so, he declared, they have been left almost entirely alone since 1874 when Elijah Davidson, a hunter trailing a bear, found the little doorway in the face of a marble cliff.

Joaquin Miller
Poet Laureate of the Sierras
Explored the Wondrous Marble Halls of Oregon

Chandler B. Watson, a geologist and all-around learned man of Ashland, Oregon, was also a lawyer and a county judge. He came to Miller one summer and said:

Look here! That thing over there under the line between the two states is not a cave at all; it is a succession of marble grottoes; grotto on top of grotto, four or five stories high and from five to ten miles deep. I have been there twice and know more about this wondrous place than anyone else, and yet I know next to nothing about it, as yet. Come, let us go together and look at it.

Miller protested that he didn't like caves saying:

One great trouble in these trips is to get men of learning and good sense who will stick, men who are not afraid of work or weariness, cold, heat or hunger; and there are not three men in a thousand of this sort. Therefore, make your party as small as possible. Aye, brave enough, bright enough, most of them too bright. You don't want uncommon sense on a trip of this kind, but plain quiet common sense and education, that is all. 'This world, says Carlyle. 'is peopled with nine hundred million folk, most of them fools.'

After searching awhile, Miller chose Jefferson Myers the founder of the Lewis and Clark Exposition (Portland 1905). At first Myers delayed his decision but after two months of entreaty he agreed. At an agreed time, Miller, Watson and Myers met on the Rogue River. For equipment they carried compass, lines of twine, instruments, blankets, books and maps, candles, matches, etc. Miller wrote:

I first had our commissary to write down:
Three sides of bacon (after one side of bacon was argued up to three sides)
Two books of fish hooks and flies, fishing poles with reels
Tea, Coffee, Beans, Butter, Bread, Flour
Canned fruits, sodas.

After traveling to the base of the mountain in a stage coach, they transferred to pack and saddle horses for the last steep miles to the caves. Joaquin Miller:

We could see snow, this tenth day of August away up through the tree tops at the head of the stream, and the learned geologist [Watson] said he thought maybe it might be a mountain of marble. This kept our eyes and ideas constantly in the tree tops and we were again climbing and climbing as if to overtake the evening star, until finally we pitched camp at the mouth of the marble cavern – still in the continuous woods. It is a stately and most impressive place.

The high marble front of the woodhung mountain is mantled with heavy yellow moss, as if with a garment of limitless gold. The handiwork of God is surely visible in its majestic construction.

F. M. Nickerson, of Kerbyville, a cave guide, had been summoned to meet the party at the caves.

> Nickerson and Kincaid are, perhaps the only men who are thoroughly familiar with these underground passages....
> —Chandler B. Watson 1907

Immediately after arrival and dropping the packs from the animals, the trio entered the marble cliff through the "peephole" of an entrance. The continuous breeze rushing toward them from the dark interior promptly snuffed out their candles. They also carried a railroad lantern that had a wire bail handle. Its stout frame protected the flame therefore the light was unaffected by the wind. There was water underfoot – the River Styx. They walked erect for awhile then for a time almost knee deep in the water "a sparkling stream as cold as the Klondike." Soon however, the select group was bending very low and their pace forced to go slowly while going through the low areas with very hard and rocky ceiling. Shortly thereafter they became erect again. Soon they were climbing a ladder. On another level, they encountered water roaring down a steep angle of forty-five degrees and there it joined another stream running straight west.

Miller compared what he had learned to Solomon's Temple with its adjacent ghostly ghost chambers:

The main hall here is more than three hundred feet long, nearly one hundred feet high and quite broad to say nothing of the lessor chambers to the right and to the left in flats or levels, both above and below the colossal Solomon's Temple with its Holy of Holies. These marble halls of Oregon I repeat, are not yet half way discovered or explored and they will not be for years and years to come.

Miller, discussing his venture after the trip, related that soon after the 1874 discovery of the caves by Elijah Davidson, parties soon began to explore the caves but that the entry into the caves was still generally inaccessible to the public on account of there being only a primitive trail up the mountain. Even though people visited the place...

...the miserable means of reaching this marvel of nature causes not more than one hundred people of all sorts make their way there in an entire year, at least this is what the guides assert and the two men we were fortunate enough to have with us are not illiterate boors, but real lovers of nature and have spent most of their lives here. The older of the two, Frank Nickerson, was formerly a school teacher and clerk of the county but falling in love with these marble steeps and terraces he has hovered about them for fully a quarter of a century. Nickerson is a sort of sawed-off John Muir. The other guide, John Kincaid, has cattle, a farm, a house full of babies and he won our hearts one day by calling about him his herd of high-bred hornless cows that came tearing through the trees as far as they could hear his piercing notes. A lick of salt was the secret. It is safe to say that a man who has won the good will of beasts is a pretty safe guide in the day of danger. For plenty of danger there is in these tortuous interiors.

The guides, Nickerson and Kincaid, asserted that the caves were almost inaccessible and hard to work in – and dangerous even to get a photograph – or to make one's way through the tortuous interior.

Miller recollected the places of visit included the Bottomless Pit, Nick's Slide, Roosevelt's Ride. He also remembered the Devil's Backbone ...

...sharp marble ridge on which you hitch yourself along with a leg dangling down each side while your head knocks the sharp pendant stalactites at nearly every hitch. But you must keep your seat for either side of the hog's back or ridge seems bottomless although you can hear the movement of water far below.

Miller's Thoughts About Paradise Lost

Miller was most direct about what he thought about the intriguing Paradise Lost declaring:

Paradise Lost is a creepy place. Keep out of it! We got in there by accident or to be frank about it, we got lost and so it was that we put the sign "Paradise Lost." It is truly a wonderful place but as there are plenty and to spare of other wonderful places you should give it a wide berth; for at least you will have to turn back, after getting in, and as it is very dangerous there is no sense in taking the same risk twice.

About getting lost a second time:

Miller described how he and the others had stayed in the cave longer than they planned, and by now they were concerned for their dog which had been left behind. Nickerson, who seemed to be in a great haste to get to the outside, took the team of explorers on a cutoff he believed to be a shortcut but alas! There

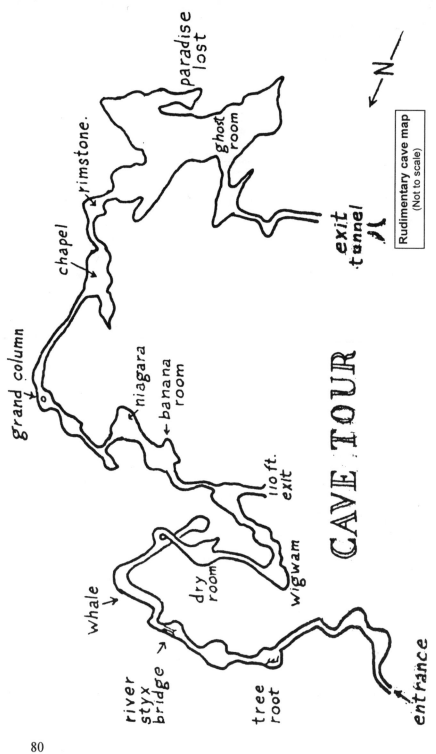

CAVE TOUR

Rudimentary cave map
(Not to scale)

N

paradise lost
ghost room
rimstone
chapel
grand column
niagara
banana room
110 ft. exit
wigwam
dry room
whale
river styx bridge
tree root
entrance
exit tunnel

80

was no outlet. Lost again! Nickerson tried this way then that way but finally, exhausted, all the men sat for a rest and to consider what to do. Try to go back? Where was "back"?

Nickerson had saved himself from a fall of two hundred feet simply by being tall enough to reach the ceiling with his hand, and Miller "cooned" under a cliff at the risk of his life and felt certain he could not turn around without slipping off into the chasm below. Miller wrote that he was just then thinking of all the good things that had passed through his life and wishing the whole marble show a permanent place in sheol. He was ready to get out of the caves!

Just then the little dog that had been left tethered outside the cave came bounding to his master, guide Kincaid, barking at every jump and shaking his dripping body with delight.

Here was a revelation: This dog had not climbed any ladders. He had kept on right up the stream and then found his way to the men through unknown passages. With his arrival, the dreary moods of the little group took full energy as if from a newly charged battery.

The group could follow the dog's wet paw tracks and get out. They went out.

That night, in the tent huddled around the railroad lantern, after considerable discussion, the geologist, Watson, concluded that the trip would forever be incomplete in the minds of these explorers if the men did not go back into the cave, loaded with Roman candles, to determine where the connection might be between the Bottomless Pit and the place where the dog had entered the cave.

In the morning, after a hearty breakfast of boiled oatmeal and strong coffee, all but Miller went back into the cave. Miller was to stay at the entrance to listen and to look. In the time that elapsed from the men's entry until their exit, he heard no cave-related sounds. A controlling manner employed by the explorers was to light Roman candles, whose acrid odor surely could not be missed, and would pour out of the cave as if the men were celebrating the 4th of July. Miller reasoned that the harsh smoke must have followed the River Styx straight as a string laid on the floor for guidance, as the men at the place where the candle had been lit explained that its smoke did not rise in their faces or cause them any inconvenience.

The exploring party had torn down a toll gate and ticket office shack that had been set up near the orifice of the cave by someone unidentified.

A list was made by Myers and Watson of chambers and places of special delight and places of danger.

First Floor — (Lower entry) River Styx, Watson's Gorge, Davidson's Bear Pit, Rachel's Well, Roosevelt's Ride, Paradise Lost, Moses' Chamber, Joseph's Tomb.

Second Floor — (Upper entry) Shark's Jaw, Nick's Bed Chamber, Queen's Place, King's Place, Pillar Room, King's Highway, Niagara Falls, Windy Passage, Theatrical Stage, The Star Chamber, Washington's Statue, Nick's slide.

(Dangerous: Bottomless Pit, Treasurer's Chamber.

Third Floor — Golden Stairway, Jefferson Myers' Room, Solomon's Temple (350 x 150 x 80) Ghost Chamber, Kincaid's Dance Hall, Holy of Holies.

Fourth Floor — Oregon Loft (unexplored).

◇

Memorial marker to Elijah Davidson's discovery of the Oregon Caves. Find this monument on trail between Chalet and cave entrance.

Dick Rowley (left) who conducted early tours through the Oregon Caves, and Elijah Davidson who discovered the caves. They were life-long friends.

THE OREGON CAVES

QUEER FORMATIONS
RESEMBLING
HUGE HIBISCUS BLOSSOMS

SISKIYOU
NATIONAL FOREST

THE OREGON CAVES

AT THE ENTRANCE TO
THE OREGON CAVES

SISKIYOU
ATIONAL FOREST

Covers of pamphlet about the Oregon Caves of early 1920's. Note rubber stamp of "May 6, 1924" the date on which the Connecticut State Library accessioned the pamphlet into its collection. Authors borrowed the original from the library to make this reproduction in 1998.

Guides stand in entrance to the caves.
(Picture from pamphlet shown on page 85)

Old cave exit.
(Picture from pamphlet shown on page 85)

"Niagara Falls"
(Picture (TOP) from pamphlet shown on page 85)
(LOWER) First known picture of government sign proclaiming the Oregon Caves National Monument. The print reads, in part, that a fine of "not more than $100 or be imprisoned for a period of not more than 10 days.... Only the Secretary of Agriculture can permit the removal from or ... of objects in these caves [by direction of] forest supervisor Fromme...Oregon"

Elijah Jones Davidson
1849 – 1927
At age 25, he discovered the Oregon Caves
on November 12, 1874 while on a hunting trip.

Pamphlet of undiscovered date but probably in 1920's.

Mountain, Forest and Stream, Oregon Caves Road

Promotional text from late 1930's brochure:

The Oregon Caves, "Marble Halls of Oregon" as they are some-times called, comprise a series of immense chambers connected by natural passages and extending hundreds of feet into the heart of Cave Mountain.

From the mouth of the Caves, flows a sparkling stream of ice cold water. The chambers are of marble with stalactites and stalagmites which Nature's Artists have been scores of centuries in forming. Many fantastic shapes are found resembling marble statuary. A few of the many chambers

Headquarters Building, Dining Room and Office

viewed by the visitors are: The Wigwam, Petrified Forest, Neptune's Grotto, the King's Palace, Ghost Chamber, Dante's Inferno, The Menagerie, and Paradise Lost. Every step of the way leads to new wonders. As one emerges from the Caverns the almost invariable expression is: "The Caves are grand beyond by greatest expectations."

The Caves are located in the heart of the Siskiyous, 4,000 feet above the sea. They are 50 miles from Grants Pass and are reached by a good automobile road. From Grants Pass the route lies south over the Redwood Highway toward Crescent City for 32 miles. Road signs point the way.

An Information Bureau and Store at the Grayback bridge, seven and one-half miles from the Caves, is conducted by the Oregon Caves management and reservations by telephone to the Caves for lodging accommodations and for meals may be made.

The last seven and a half miles is over a scenic government highway. This road has a maximum grade of 6 percent and winds up the mountain side through a wonderful foresight of pine and fir. The trip alone would well repay one for the time spent. A commodious auto parking place has been provided near the caves for all autos. The temperature at the Caves is delightfully cool but not cold. There are no mosquitoes.

Courteous guides make regular trips through Caves at 9 and 10 a.m., at 1 and 3:30 p.m. and at other hours between 8 a.m. and 4 p.m. when a sufficient number of visitors for a usual party is at hand. A party, under one guide, is not permitted to exceed 16 people.

Regular guide service commences May 15 and closes October 15. After June 15, and until September 1, a regular trip will also be made at 7 p.m. Special guide service by arrangement.

The route through the Oregon Caves has been fully explored and traversed by more than 60,000 people without a single accident. The walls of the Caves are of solid marble rock and have stood unchanged for ages.

Daily Rates — European Plan (meals extra)
Tent houses   1 person $1.50
Tent houses   2 persons $2.50
Cottages $3.00 bath & toilet - 2 people $5.00

Meals:
Breakfast 75¢   Lunch $1.00   Dinner $1.00
Special weekly rates American Plan (with meals)

Coast Auto Line Daily Stages are operated
from Grants Pass, Ore. and Crescent City, Calif.
    Leave Grants Pass 9:15 a.m. and 2 p.m.
    Leave Crescent City 8 a.m. and 1 p.m.
Long distance telephone and telegraph service.

For Information Address Oregon Caves Resort,
George C. Sabin, General Manager, Oregon Caves, Oregon.

"AROUND THE CAMPFIRE"

Walter C Burch, right, and Homer D. Harkness opened the Oregon Caves as a tourist spot in 1885. Burch was in charge while his partner was busy running the stage stop at Grave Creek. Here the men play cards in a photo taken almost 100 years ago in Grants Pass.

At the caves is a headquarters building of Swiss Architecture with dining room and kitchen in charge of members of the home economics department of the Oregon Agricultural College, Corvallis. A building in charge of an agreeable and competent lady has been provided for children too small for a Cave trip. This building was planned to be attractive to little folks and you may find that they are not willing to leave when you are ready to depart.

Cottages and tent houses are furnished with high-grade beds. Hot and cold spring water is piped to each cottage and each has private bath and toilet. Electric lights within buildings and tent houses, also about the grounds. A huge camp fire for those who enjoy the evening with song and story is a regular evening feature.

Those who spend evenings at the Oregon Caves among the pines, will long remember it as a land of enchantment.

You Should Visit This Scenic Wonder of Oregon

Townsend's Big-eared Bat
(*Plecotus townsendii*)

Chapter 4
Wildlife Abounds at
Oregon Caves National Monument.

Everyday type animals as those found in many forests –
squirrels, chipmunks, skunks, deer, bear, cougar and the like –
even slugs and snails – all require the sun, trees, grasses,
moderate climate, and the food-chain that develops in these
conditions, for survival.

In the old growth forest of the type found in the Oregon
Caves National Monument, these types of creatures depend on a
set of characteristics unique to the woods. The squirrel feeds on
seeds of large mature conifers. Small animals may burrow in the
earth for their homes while some larger animals can sleep curled
in the grass or as some do, on the limbs of trees. In the food
chain, some larger animals attack and eat some of the smaller
animals.

As visitors picnic or even walk across a parking lot you may
be approached by a cute little chipmunk or a raucous Stellar Jay.
They beg or simply look hungry. Scraps from a lunch seem an
easy treat to these moochers. With tidbit in fingers, you reach
down and tempt the beggars. Moments later the little creature is
eating out of your hand. What a photo opportunity! These beggars can become aggressive and obnoxious. The rascal mistakes

your finger for one of those tempting morsels you so graciously offered. You howl with the shock of having been bitten, then face the possibility of a long series of shots for rabies and the melancholy memory of your day at the Oregon Caves National Monument. People become the losers in the seemingly innocent offer of tidbits to the animals.

Many are the stories of bears living in caves. Bears might hole up in a cave for a nap, or wander in for a little exploring, or seek refuge in a cave if being chased, but bears do their real living away from caves for there is nothing for a bear to eat in a cave and bears cannot see in the dark.

Slugs and snails live in the Oregon Caves and can be found in some of the deepest parts of the cave. The rasping jaws of slugs and snails have many tiny teeth used to scrape off cave algae against a horny plate in the upper part of the mouth. The brownish banana slug is the most often seen slug both above and below ground on the Monument.

The Pacific Giant salamander finds a moist home in the cave away from dryness, starvation or cold outside. In the summertime, the cave temperatures lowers the salamander's metabolism so it doesn't have to eat as often. It can eat small birds but in the cave it may be feeding on small invertebrates that in turn eat moss and algae that grows by the lights. This is the world's largest salamander and one of the few that make sounds. Its low-pitched rattle and explosive cry resemble a barking dog.

Trogloxene (cave visitors), are often seen and stay awhile, but are not permanent residents in caves. Bats, crickets, bushy-tailed woodrats and hibernating bears are *trogloxenes*. Because today there are heavy gates on all accesses to the Oregon Caves, it would be nearly impossible for bears to get inside.

Nevertheless, there are animals that live in the cave full time but visitors probably will not see these unless one gets quite far into the caves where it is really dark. *Troglophiles* (cave lovers) have adapted to live in caves but can live on the surface as well. Bats and bushy-tailed woodrats are *troglophiles*. Bats are usually deep in the cave beyond the tour routes. If bats are seen by a guide, the guide will point them out.

True cave dwellers are called *troglobites* and nearly always spend their entire life cycle in caves. In the Oregon Caves these include albino millipedes and certain springtails. A low energy cave food chain including producers (bacteria and fungus) form moonmilk, *omnivore*, a cave cricket, and *camivore* a harvestman commonly called "daddy long legs" live there.

Many *troglobites* live in perpetual darkness. Some are very light color or even white, having lost their color as they don't need color to attract mates or as camouflage to protect themselves from predators. Another adaptation to cave darkness is having longer legs and antennae which have many "sense" organs, as *troglobites* depend on these for touch and feeling to help them locate food and to find mates.

Bats at Monument

Townsend's big-eared bat is the most common bat in the Oregon Caves. Bats can navigate in total darkness because they emit sound waves, the waves then reflect off objects in their path and echo back to the bat's listening system. This radar-like system is called echolocation. This navigating manner helps bats find insects, a bat's major food source, in the dark.

Bats are the subjects of stories and legends and are often assigned the role of the villain. In popular movies and articles, bats are considered to be dangerous and threatening.

Are bats truly evil or just the victims of a bad reputation?

Much of the bat's negative standing is due to peoples' unfamiliarity with the job bats perform in the environment. Bats are found world-wide except in Antarctica. Being nocturnal or active mostly at night, bats are not easily studied. Bats are a most diverse group with more identified species than any other group of animals.

Bats' dietary habits are quite varied and are of significant economic importance to man. Fruit eating bats, in the tropics, may help distribute seeds far from their parent plants. Nectar feeding bats, in the southeastern United States, help pollinate plants. Some plants that depend on bats to reproduce include the

(—continued on page 100)

Cave centipede.

Just About Everyone Likes a "Bear" Story Especially as a Bear Played a Most Important Part in the Discovery of the Oregon Caves

The old gent was a man of few words.

"Found fresh bear tracks
   Turned dogs loose
      After while got a little bark
         After long while got as lot of barks
            Dogs had bear treed
               We got to tree just after dark
                  Looked above
                     Saw something big and black
                        Shot into tree
                           Got growl
                              Shot again
                                 Got a little blood
                                    Shot third time
                                       Got big shower of
                                          huckleberries"!

—Adapted from *Curry County Echoes*. Curry Country Historical Society.
Gold Beach, Ore. Vol. 26. No. 1. January 1998.

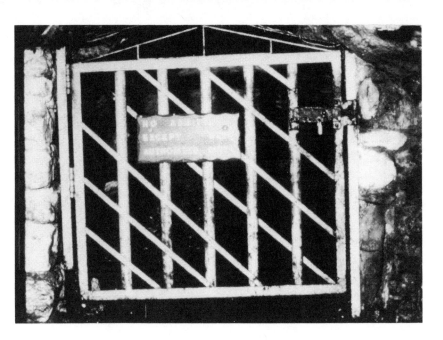

Security gates. (TOP) Old style gate . Sign reads "NO ADMITTANCE EXCEPT AUTHORIZED GUIDES" did not permit bats to fly through. (LOWER) New type gates, preserves the rule of no persons to enter without certified guide but allows bats access.

saguaro cactus, agave from which Tequila is made, cashew plants and some bananas.

All the bats living within the Oregon Caves National Monument feed on insects. Many of the insects eaten by bats, such as moths and beetles, are responsible for damage to crops therefore bats are a natural control against insects.

Bats have assisted in many scientific studies. Examina-tion of echolocation, used by insect eating bats to locate prey, has improved man's radar systems. Medical research has in-cluded bats. The study of the ability of some bats to store sperm and delay fertilization has contributed to medical knowledge of fertility and birth control, as well as organ rejection in humans. An-alysis of red blood cell production and scrutiny of blood flow through the thin membranes of a bat's wings have assisted in understanding man's blood systems.

Black-tailed deer at Oregon Caves National Monument

> Bats, like all mammals, can have rabies but that incidence is found to be less than half of one percent of all bats. More people contract rabies from the family dog than from bats. This is because a bat's mouth is constructed for crunching insect shells – not for biting through human skin.

The fact is bats are in much greater danger from humans than humans are of bats. Due to fear and ignorance, the lives of numerous bats are in jeopardy every day as bat habitats and individual bats are destroyed.

At least eight species of bats make the Oregon Caves their part-time roost. Most of these bats use the cave just at night, roosting in nearby buildings, trees or rock crevices during the day. Unlighted cave areas away from the main tour passages are used by the few daytime bat inhabitants. As the result of a study in the late 1970's, eighty percent of the bats in the Oregon Caves were discovered to be male.

During a bat population survey at Oregon Caves National Monument in 1982, a bat was captured that had been tagged during a 1958 survey. That bat, a Long-eared Myotis, must have been at least 24 years old! Many bats live to between 15 to 18 years old.

So what of the wicked and evil deeds thought to be associated with bats? Considering the many bats sharing the world with people, man and bats rarely cross paths and when they do, the outcome is seldom adverse.

The lives of bats and humans are entwined in ways hard to imagine. What people eat, modern medical and technological breakthroughs, entertainment, and the quality of life may be affected by the continued survival of some "ugly" misunderstood nightflying creatures called bats. ◇

> **Pack rats** can follow their own urine trail to navigate in the total darkness of a cave.

What Lives in the Oregon Caves is Hot Topic
New Species Found at Oregon Caves

What's a *Grylloblatid*?

Compared to most surface environments, most caves offer little food for its insect inhabitants. Caves usually lack much wind, light, freeze-thaw cycles, or organics. Therefore, fragile minerals and species with low metabolisms normally thrive underground. Foot traffic, lights, clothing lint, tunnels and vandalism have high energy and food impacts on caves. Visitors, or altered airflow bring in skin flakes, dust, spores, or detergent-rich lint, all of which foster plant growth that is not natural in the cave. In Oregon Caves, Carlsbad Caverns and probably many other commercialized caves, alien animal communities have developed on lint deposits and exotic plants. Such an unnatural increase in food can cause what is termed the "paradox of enrichment." This is where surface-adapted insects move in and out compete with smaller and slower moving cave-adapted insects. The extinction rate from these impacts depends in part on whether caves are evolutionary "islands" or whether most cave bugs come from small cracks surrounding the cave. Finding out which of these models best applies to cave communities is a hot topic of cave research.

Year around baselines are needed to understand the evolution of cave communities and the human-caused impacts on them. Unfortunately, until recently, all that was known about Oregon Caves fauna were miscellaneous notes such as "small white spider seen in Neptune's Grotto."

The first micro-invertebrate survey of the Oregon Caves began in late August of 1992. Eighteen pit traps were placed in the cave so as to help determine the effects of cave entrances, humidity, and nearness to the cave trail on cave populations and species composition. Limburger cheese was the bait and has already yielded at least 25 species.

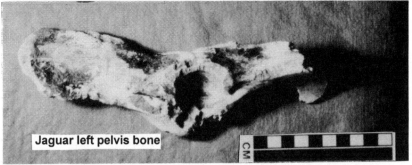
Jaguar left pelvis bone

A primitive insect called a *gryllobatid* was found in November. It is likely to be a new species found nowhere else in the world.

Gryllobatids are primitive insects found mostly on glaciated or formerly glaciated areas. Around 12,000 years ago, glaciers were on the move within about one mile of the Oregon Caves. The gryllobatid is a glacial relic which retreated to the cold and wet cave when the climate above ground became warmer and drier.

A Jaguar in the Oregon Caves?

While placing survey markers for a mapping project, cave researcher Steve Knutson discovered some animal bones buried in a small gravel-filled passage near the Ghost Room of the cave. In August 1995, a paleontologist assisted in digging for some of the bones and identified them as rare fossil jaguar bones.

This may be the most complete fossil jaguar skeleton ever found. Not only does the find interest paleontologists, it is also useful to geologists in estimating the minimum age of the cave. If only a few bones had been found, those bones could have been buried and then later washed into a much younger Oregon Caves. However, the completeness of the skeleton suggests that this jaguar entered the cave in one piece. Thus, the cave must be at least as old as the jaguar. Based on the size of the bones, this jaguar probably lived between 15,000 to 40,000, years ago. The bones are larger than those of present day jaguars but smaller than some other Pleistocene fossil jaguars found elsewhere in North America. This animal probably lived toward the end of the last Ice Age when the size of jaguars decreased.

Caves can preserve things for long periods of time because of the constant temperature and slow rates of change. ◇

Vintage of the automobiles indicate the picture is mid-to-late-1940's. Chateau on left, Chalet in rear. There is no provision at the National Monument for horses at the present time.

104

Chapter 5
Civilian Conservation Corps (CCC)
At Oregon Caves National Monument

The "CCC" as it was called, was organized during the Great Depression as one of President Franklin D. Roosevelt's "New Deal" programs. Its purpose was a means for putting unemployed young unmarried men to work on national conservation projects. The work included planting trees on public lands, fighting forest fires, maintaining forest roads and trails, etc. The men lived in work camps in a semi-military manner, with Army officers in charge. These men earned $1 a day plus food, housing and medical requirements provided by the Army. The program ran from 1933 until the start of World War II being disbanded in 1942. At its peak, there were about half-a-million men enrolled.

Public Restroom and checking office at the monument's parking lot.

Camp Oregon Caves was a CCC camp established at the base of the mountain. These men did trail clearing in the National Monument and provided work parties in the caves.

In 1936, there were enough men at the camp to require seven cooks. All of the men wore two-piece blue denim army fatigue suits. As transportation to town for the men was *shanks mare* (walking), most stayed in camp including on weekends. The National Park Service Rangers and Forest Service personnel provided nature talks and from time-to-time brought in a 16mm sound movie projector with Hollywood movies. For a screen, the movies were projected on a bed sheet hung between two trees.

A major cave project was the finishing of the exit tunnel (including blasting). Other work was with widening passages, removing "low bridge" head-bumping low ceilings, putting in railings, cementing rocks in place along trails, installing metal stairs and keeping the caves clean. A water pipe in the cave was converted for carrying compressed air for use on air drills. One writer, Finch, agreed that "some work should be done to improve dangerous places" but he thought the "picturesque squeezes and low bridges should be left." (Some were.)

Surface projects included keeping roads clear, widening the narrow 900-foot long road between the Chateau and lower (large) parking lot, digging out stumps from the parking lot, and conservation work of removing fire-hazard brush from around the buildings. The men were rotated between inside and outdoor work.

CCC major construction was a 38,000 gallon fresh water reservoir. They built the campfire circle. The men constructed the tool shed for the ranger now used as a concessionaire garage. The 8,000-feet of water pipe was hauled uphill by block and tackle by men walking down hill pulling the tow line that ran through a pulley at the top.

The 1934 telephone line of 11.7 miles was a CCC project. The materials cost only $880. The cumulative costs for trail work was $13,100 which included surface oiling to hold down dust. The Big Tree Trail was rerouted to bring materials up the pipeline route.

At a cost of $779, the CCC men built picnic grounds, tables and benches and installed sanitation. An one-and-one-half year long project was the hand placement of rocks in the retaining walls around the lodge (Chateau). The bronze plaques at the entrance of the Monument replaced temporary wooden signs.

Projects in the general area included a 75-foot long bridge over Sucker Creek, a small dam on Lake Creek, a ten acres topographic survey, 2.5 acres of camp ground improvement. The men placed 700-feet of water pipe in the camp ground and built a community house. The work on the camp site was finished with planting 250 trees and shrubs.

Courses taught in the CCC camps were designed to help men obtain jobs after leaving the camps. Before the start of World War II, some infantry drill exercises, without rifles, were being taught and men learned to march. With the outbreak of World War II in the Pacific with the Japanese attack on Pearl Harbor, the CCC was terminated as men either volunte-ered or were drafted into the military services or found jobs in the defense industry.

With the loss of the CCC manpower, maintenance work in all National Parks, including in the Oregon Caves National Monument, suffered dramatically. ◇

Tall Bear Story

It was alleged that one of the CCC boys put up a warning sign, which had very small print, on a tree by the forest trail. It merely advised: "If you can read this sign you're standing next to a bear trap."

—Adapted from *Curry County Echoes*. Curry Country Historical Society. Gold Beach, Ore. Vol. 26. No. 1. January 1998

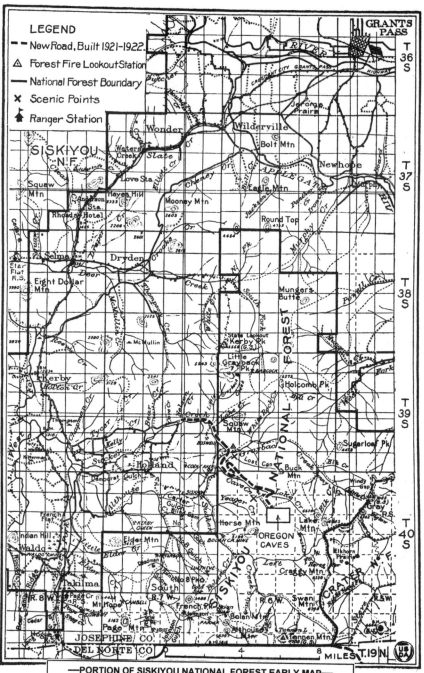

—PORTION OF SISKIYOU NATIONAL FOREST EARLY MAP—
ROGUE RIVER NATIONAL FOREST WAS THEN KNOWN AS CRATER
NATIONAL FOREST NOTED NEAR LOWER RIGHT CORNER. A SHARP
EYE CAN PICK OUT THE CALIFORNIA & OREGON COAST RAILROAD
--+---+---+---+---+- RUNNING SOUTHWEST FROM GRANTS PASS

Chapter 6
Visiting the Oregon Caves Today

> At the present time, there is no entry fee to visit the Oregon Caves National Monument which is operated by the National Park Service. However, to tour the caves, visitors pay a fee for certified guide service and cave interpretation by the guides. For security, all access to the caves is through locked gates. No person is allowed in the caves without a certified guide.

Particulars about the National Monument and the Oregon Caves, including schedules of operations, entertainment during summer months, and campgrounds, can be obtained at the Illinois Valley Visitors and Information Center in Cave Junction, on Highway 46 half-a-block from the turn from Highway 199, or at the Information Booth in the parking lot on the monument.

Visitors with trailers, including 5th-wheel units, are advised to drop their hauls at the Information Center parking lot as there is no parking space at the Monument, and no way to turn the larger vehicles, including most recreational vehicles. Inquire at Illinois Valley Visitor Center about summer season shuttle busses to the Monument (fee). The drive from Cave Junction to the National Monument parking lot is 20 miles – about 40 minutes – nearly half the distance over a steep mountain road with tight curves. The parking area is limited to about 100 automobile-size vehicles. Gasoline is not available beyond Cave Junction, the city being a full service center including gasoline, food, motels, grocery stores, post office, Josephine County Sheriff's office, laundro-mats, lawyers, public library, etc.

Usual driving time to Cave Junction from Crescent City in California is about 90-minutes. The trip from Grants Pass to Cave Junction is about 25-minutes.

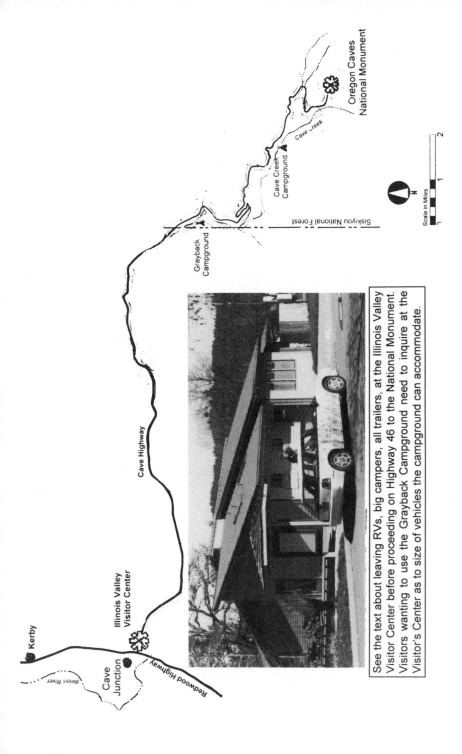

See the text about leaving RVs, big campers, all trailers, at the Illinois Valley Visitor Center before proceeding on Highway 46 to the National Monument. Visitors wanting to use the Grayback Campground need to inquire at the Visitor's Center as to size of vehicles the campground can accommodate.

Oregon Caves National Monument

Cave Creek

Cave Creek Campground

Siskiyou National Forest

Grayback Campground

Cave Highway

Illinois Valley Visitor Center

Kerby

Cave Junction

Illinois River

Redwood Highway

N

Scale in Miles

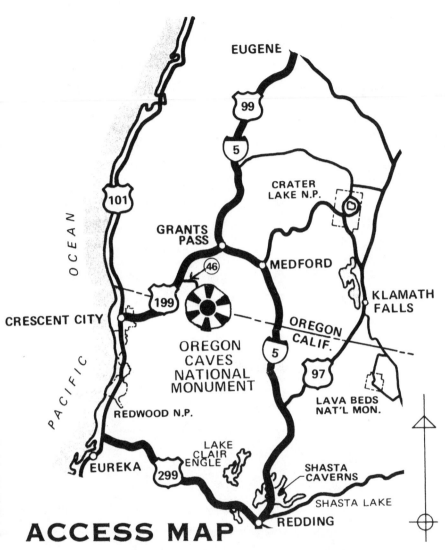

ACCESS MAP
OREGON CAVES NATIONAL MONUMENT

(TOP) **Bronze plaque near entrance to the caves.**
(LOWER) **Tour group heads toward cave entrance.**

At the monument, there is a 900-foot walk between the parking lot and the concessionaire's operations which includes the gift shop, the Chateau (overnight accommodations and food services in summer months) and assembly area for tours into the caves. Parking at the Chateau is restricted to registered guests at the Chateau.

Summers in the Illinois Valley can be quite warm with the thermometer often rising into the high 90's and as much as 102 Fahrenheit at Cave Junction's 1,357 elevation. (It is cooler at 4,000 feet elevation at the National Monument.) In town, winters are often gray and wet. On the mountain, the average *yearly* snowfall is about 14 *feet* with as much as 36-inches accumulated near the cave entrance. During winter, due to the possibility of snow and ice on Highway 46 for the final eight miles up the mountain to the parking lot near the caves, tire chains are advised realizing that although it may be only raining in the valley it can be snowing at the Monument. The Caves Highway is not usually patrolled in winter.

———

Chapter 6 A
Visiting the Oregon Caves Today
What to Expect

Persons visiting the Oregon Caves National Monument need not enter the caves, but the caves are the featured attraction.

There are seasonal picnic facilities, evening programs, and several hiking trails.   Private campgrounds operate along highway 46 in the Siskiyou National Forest. (The National Monument is within the National Forest.)

Guided tours of the Oregon Caves are offered year around, except Thanksgiving and Christmas. The caves are closed for short periods in some winters for special renovation.

Parties of visitors are escorted through 0.6 mile of awesome marble cave passages and caverns. The hikes through the caves

(TOP) **Illinois Valley Visitor's Center in Cave Junction.** (LOWER) **All-paved highway 46 from Cave Junction to the Oregon Caves National Monument.**

The paved 900-foot walkway between the parking lot and the caves. A smaller lot at the Chateau may be expanded so the monument can accommodate more cars.

can be a fun time as guides tell of the natural and cultural history that relates to the caves and their preservation. All caves contain natural hazards. In the Oregon Caves there are uneven walking surfaces, steep grades, stairs, and low head-bumping ceilings.

Cave Injuries

There are telephones along the tour route where guides can reach the headquarters office should a need arise.

- Most injuries in cave: Bumped heads to those without hard hats
- Number of carry-outs by stretcher: One per two years, or 1/200,000±
- Number of medical assistance calls: Two per year, or 2/100,000±
    —Oregon Caves National Park Service Official

Note that Dogs are not allowed in the caves or on the monument's trails.

At the monument, there is a 900-foot walk between the parking lot and the concessionaire's operations which includes the gift shop, the Chateau (overnight accommodations and food services in summer months) and assembly area for tours into the caves. Parking at the Chateau is restricted to registered guests at the Chateau.

Summers in the Illinois Valley can be quite warm with the thermometer often rising into the high 90's and as much as 102 Fahrenheit at Cave Junction's 1,357 elevation. (It is cooler at 4,000 feet elevation at the National Monument.) In town, winters are often gray and wet. On the mountain, the average *yearly* snowfall is about 14 *feet* with as much as 36-inches accumulated near the cave entrance. During winter, due to the possibility of snow and ice on Highway 46 for the final eight miles up the mountain to the parking lot near the caves, tire chains are advised realizing that although it may be only raining in the valley it can be snowing at the Monument. The Caves Highway is not usually patrolled in winter.

Hiking Trails and Water Safety Caution
Carry your own drinking water or be prepared to treat surface waters.

Big Tree Trail is 3½ miles long and takes between 2 and 3 hours. The gain in elevation is 1,100 feet. The trail goes through an old-growth forest along which is the largest diameter Douglas fir tree so far discovered in Oregon. This trail connects with a Siskiyou National Forest trail to Bigelow Lakes. To the lake and back is considered an overnight hike.

Cliff Nature Trail is one mile in length, takes about 45 minutes with an elevation gain of 400 feet.

No Name Trail is 1½ miles long and can be hiked in 45 to 60 minutes through dense forests, along mountain streams and moss-covered cliffs. Note a 400 foot elevation gain.

Special regulations pertain to children in the caves. Children must have stamina and be able to demonstrate ability to climb a set of test stairs, unassisted. This set of steps is located at the tour assembly point outside the caves. Children must be a minimum 42-inches tall. (There is no child care service at this time.)

The tour route is considered strenuous and is not recommended for those with heart, breathing or walking infirmities. The entire route – from the ticket counter, through the cave, then back along the trails after exiting the caves, is nearly one mile long. There are over 500 stair steps most being steep and some are wet. On leaving the caves, the paved trail back to the starting point is steep, a 16-percent down hill hike.

The temperature in the caves varies little over the years and stays in the low to mid-forties Fahrenheit (about 5 degrees Centigrade).* Warm clothing, even in mid-summer, is suggested as well as comfortable walking shoes with rubber or vibram soles.

Small children must be able to demonstrate ability to climb the test stairs unassisted.

---

* On an exploration by the authors, November 8, 1997, the cave temperature was 41 degrees Fahrenheit. On a visit on March 6, 1998, the temperature was still 41 F.

Certified Guide Jason Unger talks with visitors near the 110 Exit. Items to note: Hard hat, flashlight, telephone, light switch box.

There is some water on the floor in places along the tour. The cave has many electric lights, which are operated by the guide on a section-by-section basis as the tour progresses through the cave. The lights are mostly near ground level, are at irregular intervals, and are appropriately of low intensity to preserve the atmosphere spelunkers expect in a cave, yet allow one to see where one is walking. There are no lights focused on low ceilings ("low bridge") through which visitors must often stoop for passage. Wearing a hard hat is highly recommended. There seems to be almost no one known who has not bumped his head – including the certified guides – in the caves. Hard hats can be rented from the concessionaire.

The guided tour of the caves lasts about 75 minutes plus 15 to 20 minutes for the two walks to go from assembly point to the cave, then from the cave exit back to the starting point.

Taking Pictures in the Caves
—General Guidelines—

Cameras are permitted in the caves but not tripods. Visibility in the cave is so low that even seasoned photographers can not usually see anything through viewfinders. Therefore, "dead-reckoning" (point-and-shoot-and-hope) is the usual picture taking procedure.

To expect satisfactory pictures by hand-held, available-light photography even using high speed (800-1000 ASA) film is generally unfeasible due to there being no "available" light.

For the photographs made for this book by the authors, we used Kodacolor Gold MAX-type GT135 in Olympus Infinity auto-focus cameras. The flash range in the total darkness was between ten and thirty feet. Persons planning on making color photos in the caves in which people are to appear, might want to wear brightly colored clothing as drab colors tend to blend into the pitch darkness of the caves.

Camera courtesy in the caves:

When taking pictures, avoid shooting flash in the face of other visitors and the guide to avoid temporary blindness.

Frequency of Tours:

In the spring, summer and fall, tours leave in groups whenever up to 16 people have signed the log, or about every 45 minutes between tours. During May, tours are conducted between 8:30 a.m. to 5 p.m. The summer season starts with Memorial Day and ends on Labor Day with tours operating from 8 a.m. until 7 p.m. During the peak of the season, particularly on holiday weekends, tours fill more quickly than they can enter the caves therefore creating a backup. At such times, one may find himself waiting as much as a couple of hours for the next available tour.

In winter (October - April), tours start on set schedules. At this writing, those times are 9:30 and 11:30 a.m. and 1:00, 2:30 and 4:00 p.m. within the hours of 8:30 a.m. to 5 p.m. (The facilities are closed Thanksgiving Day and Christmas Day. Schedule of services may change without notice.)

Rick Rowley, guide (LEFT), **and group about ready to enter the Oregon Caves. Picture probably in 1920's.**

The costs of the tours are determined by an agreement between the National Park Service and the concessionaire. As fees are subject to change, they are not listed here.

In order to protect the features of the cave, and for the comfort of others on the tours, there are a few things that are prohibited in the caves. These include dogs, canes, crutches, walking sticks, tripods – any of which can damage the delicate cave formations. Do not bring food, chewing gum, tobacco or drinks into the caves, other than a small pocket-size personal bottle of drinking water. It is best not to hand-carry drinking water or cameras, as hands are often needed for that "steadying support" in dark and narrow passages. Cameras are best carried on neck straps. The National Park Service has no objection to small (two D-cell) flashlights in the caves.

Years ago, when Dick Rowley was the Ranger-in-Charge and Official Cave Guide, on reaching a place in the caves later named the "Wishing Post," Rowley always made the wish to always come out of the cave alive. He always did. And so do today's visitors due to the check-points and controls in the caves.

Visiting the caves can be very exciting and many are the visitors who make many return visits to the Oregon Caves National Monument. ◇

120

Chapter 6 B
Visiting the Oregon Caves Today
Touring the Cave
Editor's note: Words underscored are found in Appendix "E" (Names)

After securing a ticket at the gift shop, tour groups assemble in the arched porch area of the chalet. The certified guide meets the groups here.

Have Hard Hats Handy

Take a tip from the guide, noting that the guide wears a hard hat. Feel good about having rented a hard hat at the ticket counter as those who tour the caves wearing hard hats are certain to feel better in their heads. As beach-combers wear hats as there are seagulls up there, in the caves there are low ceilings of very hard rock up there that can dent even the hardest head. *

It's well to dress warmly even in the heat of summer as the cave temperature is a cool 41 degrees Fahrenheit. Gloves are a good idea. The cave is lighted, at intervals, nevertheless it is comforting to have a flashlight. No smoking or gum is permitted in the caves.

The guard will unlock the entrance gate and will count the number of guests as they enter the orifice. Even though the group is encouraged to stay together, the guide will look to see if there are stragglers. You will cross the River Styx on entering and quickly pass under a low ceiling into the dark of the caves.

(Persons with claustrophobia are not encouraged to make the tour however, if claustrophobia becomes apparent at this point that visitor is escorted out of the cave at the entrance gate.

Anyone who finds the tour too strenuous, can leave at the "110-Exit" – so named as it is 110 feet higher elevation than the entrance. This exit is 784-feet into the cave.)

Watson's Grotto is highlighted by solid white rock etched

---

* The earliest known head protection was a crown of straw about which there is an adventure told in Appendix B

"Niagara Falls," is an impressive example of flowstone.

"Niagara Falls," another view.
Damage on right plausibly occurred during 1891 or 1894
explorations. Note ceiling covered with "soda straws."

Cave Visitor Norm
VanManen, who
stands 6 ft 5 inches,
bends to pass under a
"low bridge" as he
walks on the steel
bridge over the River
Styx.

Tour group on the River
Styx bridge disappears
into the caves.

with drip lines before one enters <u>Petrified Gardens</u>. Visitors are encouraged not to touch the wet walls, or formations in the caves, as they are still growing. On the left are roots from the world's deepest known <u>Douglas fir tree</u>. The tree was cut in the 1960's as it was a hazard to buildings. Due to the cold climate in the cave, these roots are expected to remain for many years.

On the right side just before the <u>River Styx</u>, see the hairy rootlets on a bank of mud. The hairs are fungal threads that take in vitamins and water for the trees above the cave. Many trees allocate over two thirds of their sunlight-made food for their roots and the symbiotic fungus attached to them.

Much of the <u>River Styx</u> ran through culverts from the 1930's until 1985 when the natural stream bed was restored. Removing rubble from the river's bottom was as an archaeologist's careful dig as many cave formations were discovered during the work. Pendants and potholes mostly occur in the lower sections of the cave near the main entrance where stream flooding scoured out these features. Pendants are sharp pointed rocks hanging from the ceiling or walls. Sharp pointed ones tend to form on areas of rapid erosion such as from very acidic or turbulent water. The rapidly year-around flowing stream wore down the floor with such speed as to leave sharp points protruding above the water which did not erode away while wet.

What once were organic layers in limestone are now seen as dark graphite lines caused by acidic dew. Large crystals had room to grow in some of the ceiling cracks so did not dissolve as quickly as smaller crystals of the surrounding marble. These now stand out as palettes, which are raised stripes of <u>calcite</u> standing out by condensation of water vapor rich in carbon dioxide. When palettes intersect, this is called boxwork and can be seen in the <u>Wedding Cake Room</u>.

After crossing the <u>River Styx</u> bridge, observe the <u>flowstone</u> along the right side of the corridor. The next passage has much less flowstone because it is at right angles to the slope and therefore cannot capture as much dissolved calcite.

<u>Passageway of the Whale.</u> Gravels armored the floor and therefore kept acid water from dissolving it. The submerged passage expanded upward instead of downward. A stream gouged a

(TOP) **Rock steps to Dry Room.**
(LOWER) **Steel steps to Imagination Room.**

deep ditch in the floor – a canyon – completing a keyhole cross-section that records the cave's falling water level. Flowstone cemented with some of the gravel thereby formed an aggregate similar to concrete.

In 1989, a broken water pipe serving the old rental cabins on top of the cave caused a severe leak into the cave at the end of the passage. As the purpose in establishing the Monument was to protect the caves, the pipe, and the cabins were taken down.

The <u>Connecting Tunnel</u>. Once claystone, this dark rock was baked into argillite, a harder stone and more metamorphosed. Like toothpaste, flakes of mica slid over one another and flowed along tilted rock layers. It was so hot that the argillite recrystallized the surrounding rock destroying the graphite lines in the marble. Iron from the argillite and calcium from the marble mixed to form greenish actinolite, a mineral that needs both elements. Since water doesn't go through argillite very easily this may be why the adjacent <u>Dry Room</u> receives so little water and has so few formations.

<u>Imagination Room.</u> Cave ghosts are white, rounded images on the ceiling, the remains of formations dissolved away by acidic dew. Cave ghosts and boxwork occur high in the cave because warm air rises and condenses on the cold ceilings. Heat inside the earth warms the bottom part of the cave two degrees warmer than it is 400 feet higher in the cave. The warm air brings up from the bottom of the cave so much carbon dioxide that condensation can form carbonic acid that "eats" away calcite. This probably happened before the 110 Exit had grown large enough to flush out carbon dioxide from this area.

Rats and Spotted Owls

To the left of the stairs going up to the 110 Exit can be seen a large nest of woodrats. Humans going through the cave doesn't seem to bother them much but when they become excited or alarmed, woodrats drum their feet but this has never been heard here. The woodrats are safe in the cave for when outside, they account for more than half of all meals eaten by spotted owls.

At one time there were several rental cabins (TOP) situated on the hill among the trees behind the Chalet. Over the years they deteriorated and would eventually have been dismantled. When a pipe broke causing water to leak into the cave, all but one of the cabins was taken down. The remaining cabin (BELOW), now without water, is an office for the National Park Service. Highly photogenic in summer or in winter snow, this cabin if found along the path that terminates at the Chalet.

Beehive Room. Visitors enter this room by a squeeze stained black and even worn by touching. The trail was elevated in 1996 to reduce the amount of the squeeze and the impact on the flowstone.

110 Exit. A new gate with horizontal bars and slots to allow bats better passage was installed in 1989. Visitors who feel "too close" in the cave, and want to abort the tour, can leave the cave at this exit.

Banana Grove. Some of the flowstone mounds show missing plates of calcite facing the nearest entrance to the surface. These may record Ice Age frost wedging, a time when January temperatures might have been fifteen degrees colder. Only formations near cave entrances show ice damage as only those areas thawed in summer and refroze in winter.

Niagara Falls. An 1883 geology class field trip from University of Oregon signed their names here. Over the next 25 years, a very thin translucent layer of flowstone formed over the signatures.

The Queen's Chamber

A 1923 view. There does not appear to be any change in the last 75 years

Soda Straw. This is a small, hollow stalactite from which drops of water descend. Conceivably the fastest growing soda straw in the Oregon Caves shows an inch of growth below where it was broken off over one hundred years ago. This is above Niagara Falls. Such damage is almost permanent.

Popcorn. Near Niagara Falls is a section of bumpy cave popcorn on the right of the stalagmites.

Neptune's Grotto. Stalactites, shelfstone and flowstone are more common in upper parts of the cave because that part of the cave is older. Slow drips from climate change may explain why there are more stalactites than stalagmites.

One major shelfstone area along the cave tour occurs just before going down the spiral stairs domepit. This was once a source of abundant water for creating cave pools. The domepit probably formed when an acidic waterfall cascaded down and ate away the surrounding rock after the cave had mostly drained. Even after drainage and cave decoration, some flooding occurred as evidenced by broken soda straws engulfed by new flowstone and stream gravels sandwiched as a layer of crunchy peanut butter between flowstone layers just before the Spiral Stairs.

Grand Column. The growing together of a *stalagmite* and a *stalactite* form a column. The largest column in any cave is often called the "Grand Column" of that cave. The diameter and the height of a column depends on the age of the cave and conditions present in a particular cave. Over many centuries of growth several columns that were once close together will grow together to form a wall.

Miller's Chapel. A water droplet adds a ring of calcite to a soda straw. If the central hole is plugged, water then oozes to the outside and the soda straw grows into a wide stalactite.

Ghost Room. The vertical ledge across the room is a quartz diorite dike from the Grayback Pluton. When the rising pluton cracked surrounding rocks, volcanic rocks were injected into the cracks like raisins in a pudding. The dike recrystalized the adjacent marble into contact metamorphic rock.

Grand Column

During one of the San Francisco *Examiner's* expeditions to the caves (*see* Chapter 2), a reporter wrote about the Ghost Room and its many passages:

> Nearly all the passages explored were short. They would make a few twists and turns and then lead back into the Ghost Room.
>
> Sometimes a corridor, beginning at the main hall, would loop over or under itself two or three times in a most confusing way and would re-enter the big room within 50 feet of the place where we started. This shows that the whole region in the neighborhood of the Ghost Room is one great honeycomb.

The brown squiggles on the ceiling of the Ghost Room platforms are called "vermiculations" or "clay worms."

Paradise Lost. The climbing of the long staircase to reach this attraction may be exhausting to some visitors who could by now be becoming tired from the length and irregular surface of the footpath in the cave. If one is up to the stair-climb, the sight is worth the effort. Visitors not wanting to hike the stairs, wait at

Joaquin Miller Chapel

The spectacular Paradise Lost

Stairs to Wedding Cake Room

135

Stairs in Angle Falls Arch

It's big, it's dark except for a couple of light bulbs, and it could be scary except that there are other's on the tour nearby for comfort. Crossing the Ghost Room

Coming down from Paradise Lost.

Stairs to Wedding Cake Room are enough to weary some kids thus the "test" stairs at tour assembly area.

the bottom as the guide and others will return to this point be-fore proceeding through the remainder of the cave.

Wedding Cake Room.

This chamber was earlier known as the Bridal Chamber. Cracks that guided enlargement of side passages apparently have been offset from a fault that splits the room in two. This fault probably formed as molten rock from the Grayback Pluton cooled, crystallized and shrank in size. Rock around the pluton sank along a series of faults that may have developed in the same cracks formed during the tearing apart of the ocean basin in which the marble formed. The fault shattered the sur-rounding rock. Large solution-resistant crystals of calcite filled the cracks. Acidic dew condensed on ceilings in high rooms etching more boxwork, as seen here, in those areas.

Exit Tunnel. The tunnel was blasted and dug in the 1930's to eliminate the necessity of having tour groups reverse their route then grope their way back to the 110-Exit to leave the caves.

Digging tunnels and enlarging trails created much rubble that blocked airflow in the cave and covered many formations. To restore the cave to a more natural state, the National Park Service removed nearly three million pounds of rubble – over 100,000 bucket loads – all had to be carried out of the cave by hand. Some impacts to the cave were unintended as tunnel construction

Exit Tunnel

exposed pyrite, a mineral, to oxygen. The breakdown of this
"fool's gold" forms reddish rust stains and a small amount of
sulfuric acid (the same acid found in car batteries). The acid
apparently dissolved formations further down in the cave.

An imposing contorted marble cliff greets visitors as they
leave the cave.

The walk back to the Chalet is on a steep but paved path
with a handrail.

Editor's Note: Readers may wish to review the names of rooms and other
places in the caves by referring to Appendix E: Names of Caverns,
Rooms, and Other Places on or Near Oregon Caves National Monument.

Appendix A
Dr. Thomas Condon, Geologist -
University of Oregon, Visits Caves

Letter written in 1988 by Mrs. Robert E. Dunn, a granddaughter of George W. Dunn, concerning a visit to the "Josephine Co. Caves" in 1883 by her grandfather. Its reproduction here is courtesy of Southern Oregon Historical Society.

June 17, 1988.
To Southern Oregon Historical Society, Medford, Oregon.

Dear Society:

In going through some of the things in Grandfather George W. Dunn's house at 65 Granite Street in Ashland, Oregon, we found this written by him in 1883. We found it very interesting and since not many people have had the experience, we thought you might find it interesting too.

Sincerely yours,
Mrs. Robert E. Dunn (Ashland)

--------------///---------------

Dr. Condon's Trip to the Josephine Co. Caves 1883

Doctor Thomas Condon, famed geologist and member of the faculty of University of O[regon], made it known to some of his students from Jackson County that he desired to visit the caves that had been recently discovered by one of the Davidson boys who lived on Williams Creek, a tributary of the Applegate River in Jackson County. Arrangements were made and a party to accompany him composed of the late Jim Birdsey (at that time sheriff of Jackson Co.), W. W. Cardwell, Ben B. Beekman, Frank R. Neil and George W. Dunn, students at that time attending the University of Oregon (except the sheriff).

On a date in September of 1883, it was planned to start from Jacksonville, Oregon. On an appointed day Dr. Condon (to the U of O boys "Uncle Tommy"), arrived in Jacksonville and a meeting was arranged for him to do a talk to which nearly all of Jacksonville's citi-

Thomas Condon

zens were present. He gave a splendid geological description of the formation of the geological structures and changes which the Oregon country had undergone since million of years ago. He was heartily cheered and when he sat down Mr. C. C. Beekman, the Jacksonville banker, arose and asked the Doctor how he reconciled to vast ages of which he spoke, with the account of the formation of the earth as recorded in the book of Genesis in the Holy Bible. "Ah," he [Dr. Condon] said, "the days mentioned in the Bible were long periods of time (millions of years of our time)." At the close of his address, Ben Beekman arose and explained that the Doctor was at considerable expense coming out from Eugene so he thought we should show our appreciation by presenting him with a small contribution. Whereupon the hat was passed around and the Doctor's expenses were liberally taken care of.

The next day the cave explorers set out from Jacksonville on a hot dusty and exceedingly rough trip in a ... wagon loaded with supplies (very limited) and also a saddle horse which was to be used as a pack horse after the wagon reached a dead end at the Davidson cabin on the head of Williams Creek.

From thereon there was not much of a trail to the caves. So the services of "Carty" [Carter] Davidson, as pilot and cave finder* were secured. In order to reach the caves we had to cross over Gray Back Mountain which was heavily timbered and very steep. With our camp outfit securely lashed on Barney's back (the saddle horse) we finally crossed the summit of old Gray Back and proceeded in southerly direc-

---

* The cave was discovered in 1874 by Elijah Davidson, a brother of Carter Davidson.

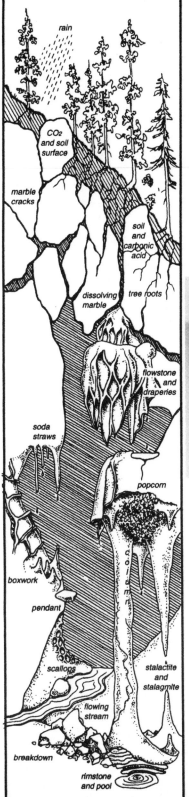

rain

CO_2 and soil surface

marble cracks

soil and carbonic acid

dissolving marble

tree roots

flowstone and draperies

soda straws

popcorn

boxwork

pendant

c o l u m n

scallops

stalactite and stalagmite

flowing stream

breakdown

rimstone and pool

(LEFT) **Cutaway sketch of typical cave formations. Dunn, in his letter, mentions that Dr. Condon "brought out 'stalactites'" as examples of the cave's decorations. (LOWER) Pictures made by the authors at the University of Oregon Geology Museum in early 1998 show object identified as from Dr. Condon's caves field trip, seems to resemble "rimstone" as shown near bottom of sketch. The top view is as the object appears in the sketch. Bottom view is underside.**

WEIGHT: 7 LBS 15 OZ.
CONDON MUSEUM STALACTITE

143

tion quite a distance where there was an open glade on which we established a camp and staked Barney out in luxuriant grass as a reward for his super horse struggle in carrying our outfit in for us.

The cave was not far aways [*sic*.], so on the next morning, armed with balls of binder twine and candles, which were to light our way into the caves and guide us out again, "Carty" soon piloted us to the mouth of the cave. It was a small opening about the size of a modern fireplace, from which a small cold stream of water headed for Sucker Creek, a tributary of the Illinois River on the Josephine Country side of "old Gray Back."

On entering the caves and lighting our candles, we soon entered a rather large opening from the ceiling of which pure white stalactites hung in various sizes and shapes. On the floor of the cave the stalag-mites were building up from the dripping of the lime impregnated water. A weird, wonderful display of millions of sparkling diamonds reflected from our candlelight. One cannot imagine how white the caves were when lit up by our feeble candles, or how dense the darkness was when the lights went out.

At that time there was no discoloration. Later, pitch torches carried by visitors made the scenery look as if one had been living therein.

We encountered many difficulties in our progress into the caves, on account of the slippery rocks, narrow passages and low ceilings. At that time no work had been done to open up new vistas or make possible easier access to the hidden beauties later discovered.

Dr. Condon brought out of the caves samples of the stalactites to add to his collections at the U of O.

In addition to the lower entrance which we first entered there was a small opening over the caves about the size of a badger hole. We decided to investigate it. Most of us were not too large diametrically speaking and managed to enter or lower ourselves a few feet where we discovered a beautiful chamber.

We had not been in long when the dim light penetrating from above suddenly blinked out. The cause: Jim Birdsey, whose belly was much larger than his head, had tried to follow the leader and only got both legs down the hole which his excessive circumference completely plugged. Jim was in a serious predicament, so were the ones exploring on hands and knees the newly discovered chamber. We were corked up neatly in a space rather not too small for slow suffocation.

Fortunately, by virtue of almost super-human strength, Jim extri-cated his legs so as to admit fresh air of which we were in dire need.

[End of narrative]

◇

144

Appendix B
Early Days at Oregon Caves – 1885

With his brother-in-law Homer D. Harkness, 26-year-old Walter C. Burch opened the caves in 1885 as a tourist attraction. In the coming season, visitors could have a guided tour of the cave by "caveman" Burch, a camping site and pasture for their horses all for one dollar for each person.

Years later Burch wrote about his experiences and before he died in 1935, he gave the paper to his son Clair W. Burch. The paper was loaned to Frank Walsh of Coos Bay for editing and publishing in the *Illinois Valley News* of Cave Junction in 1983.

It was in the fall of 1884 when Walt Burch learned about the caves which were in the mountains about 35 miles south of Grants Pass. He was staying the winter at Grave Creek but because the caves interested him, he organized an exploring party and prepared to make the trip. His companions were Charles Johnson, Samuel Harkness and F. M. Harkness.

They left Grave Creek in early November riding in a spring wagon. They went through Grants Pass and to Kerbyville. Along the way, at Sucker Creek the party was increased by the addition of George Griggs who was to be the guide. After some rough trail, the party located the caves about 4 in the afternoon – nearly dark.

Following having some food, they immediately went into the caves and spent about five hours emerging from the upper entrance which Burch described as a "very small hole to get through."

The following day Burch posted a notice listing Homer D. Harkness and himself as "locators" anticipating obtaining title under the Stone Act. The party left the site and returned to their winter quarters.

When spring arrived, Burch put together a second expedition which would build a trail following what is now called Cave Creek to the caves. These men were John Wesley Burch (Burch's father), Robert Ferguson, Perry McDaniels and another man, a veteran of the Mexican War whose name Burch did not recall. The trail they cleared was 4 1/8 mile long and took from May 14 until July 2 to complete.

The next project was to develop a pasture where visitors' horses could feed, clear a suitable area for a camp ground and to build ladders

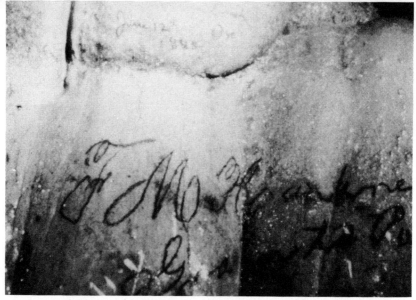

Frank M. Harkness signed his name and "Grants Pass" on cave wall during the 1884 trip of exploration. Note at top of picture faint "June 12th 1885" date of another visitor.

for use in the caves. When the work was completed in August, Burch remained at the camp ground by himself having let the others go. He stayed at the caves until the middle of October.

In the spring of 1886, Burch and McDaniels cut a new trail from the Williams Creek side over a shoulder of the mountain to the caves. With that task finished, he returned home to Grave Creek. He located Uncle Jimmie Hopkins then the two went back to the caves. As soon as they got their camp set up, they built a small cabin, which they covered with shakes (see picture page 239), then they engaged in cleanup along the earlier established trail. Hopkins, apparently tired of the labors, left. This meant that Burch would be alone. Burch recorded, " I was alone again in the most dismal canyon I had ever been in."

The year before, when he was exploring the caves, he had noticed a small opening in a wall near the Queen's Cellar. The hole emitted a heavy draft so, in 1886, he decided to drill the hole larger to see what was on the other side. He recalled:

> In all my spare time I worked on the hole by standing in a two-inch pool of ice water. That was some job to work, hard enough to keep your teeth from chattering.

Burch used small shots of powder to enlarge the hole. Finally, on August 6, he took off his outer clothing then he fed his shoes through the hole then squeezed himself through what he called "Hell's Gate" to his new discovery – a small chamber. He wrote: "Next I went down a

146

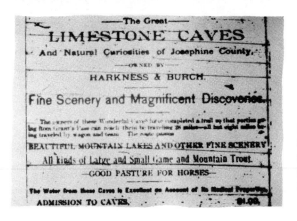

Harkness & Burch
ran this classified
advertisement.
Name of newspaper
not established.

twelve foot hole and came to the largest columns in the cave, the entrance to Diamond Hall."

Walter Burch decided it was time to get out of the cave so on his way back he found himself in Devil's Pass. Over his head was a hole so he climbed to it and holding his candle through it, he looked. The chamber "was dark [in] all [the] space except at the right were two columns – gracious ghosts. Well, that was the Ghost Chamber."

Burch wore a hat, really a crown of heavy straw, to protect his head while going through the caves. He placed his crown over the hole in the Ghost Chamber so he would know his way out. He went through the Ghost Chamber, turned to the right and saw nothing but dark, very dark space. He called the place Mammoth Chamber. He surveyed his whereabouts then, as he was standing on a great boulder...

...my candle burned my fingers. In my hurry to get out I got my directions mixed [and] I went under the bolder – then I knew I was lost!

When he regained his composure, he climbed again to the top of the boulder where, on looking about carefully, he recognized one of his markers as well as spying his straw crown. With these checkpoints established, he made his way to the outside without difficulty. Just as he reached the opening, his candle burned out.

Walt Burch was a guide in the caves for the next three years and after his 1885 experience, he carried plenty of candles and matches.

At the close of his 1886 season at the caves, he took out 420 feet of ladders and stored them for the winter under his shelter-shack.

The 1887 season had very few visitors, so by the middle of September he closed his camp and went home.

Homer Harkness and Burch held and worked the cave claim for three years all the while trying to get title to the caves from the government. They were told that their claim was denied because the land had not been surveyed thus they had to drop their claim at an out-of-pocket loss of about $1,500 in improvements. This happened in 1887. ◇

The writer of this essay is not established

Appendix C

Trip to Josephine County's Limestone Caves; The Greatest Natural Curiosities of Oregon

AT THE LIMESTONE CAVES, JOSEPHINE COUNTY — Sept. 3 (1886). There is a beautiful little creek in the canyon below the caves with waters that can be seen and heard dashing over rocks and falling over precipices ever making music. The caves are located at the head of the creek, in fact the creek flows out of the cave. There are two entrances to the caves, one being about one hundred feet higher on the bluff.

In entering the caves at the lower entrance, one passes along a hall about thirty to forty feet long and up to eight feet wide immediately over a stream of cold water. This underground creek is up to five feet wide in places, otherwise we see it only a foot or so wide and probably quite deep in the narrower places. The stream is bridged over by laying poles on either side then nailing slabs of wood on the edges creating a bridge.

At the far end of this "hall," we climb up a ladder that is about twelve feet tall which brings us into a chamber that our torches and candles reveals to be quite beautiful. In passing through these rooms, of which there are very many, one can easily hear water roaring many feet below as the water rushes toward the mouth of the caves.

We passed through a rugged hall – quite low in places– into what we call the "Elephant Chamber" where there is a perfect elephant's ear beautifully naturally carved into the wall of rock over the Devil's Backbone. This is a sharp rock with deep caverns on each side, the bottom of which can not be seen and were it not for the walk on either side being close enough to balance oneself by placing one's hands up-on them, it would be near impossible to pass over this sharp back-bone.

After passing this dangerous looking place we come to the "Devil's Pit," at any rate it seems to be a bottomless pit for we could not see its bottom.

From here we visited "Last Chance Chamber" for turning back from the earliest explorations. The first room we enter in the "New Discovery" area is named the "Hornet's Nest" for its resemblance to a hornet's nest. From there we went through an arched hall, the "Queen's

Palace," then the "Queen's Cellar," next the "Maids Parlor," and many other rooms too numerous to mention is this short communication.

Many of these rooms or chambers are the most beautiful formation of crystallized quartz and limestone that one has ever viewed. The continual dripping of water has carved out of the rock in some places all imaginable shaped icicles or resembling icicles. There are sizes that look like a straw less than one-quarter-of-an-inch diameter and up to five to six inches diameter.

The sides of these rooms are beautifully festooned with a formation resembling coral and the ceilings – beautiful beyond description in our candle light – decorated with thousands of these so-called icicles (soda straws) hanging from the ceilings sparkling and glistening like so many diamonds.

Some of the rooms have pools or small lakes of ice water, and nature has beautifully and artistically turned and carved columns which extend from floor to ceiling. The base of some columns is about ten inches diameter and looks as if they had been placed there to support the ceilings.

It is impossible to describe these great natural curiosities that God has given us, and there is no doubt but this will ere long be the grandest summer resort in Oregon. It cannot be surpassed even by the Mammoth Caves of Kentucky for beauty and grandeur. All that is needed to make this place a popular resort is a good road to it.

—Based on an article in the Grants Pass Courier September 3, 1886.

Tall Bear Story

Recalling the Elijah Davidson bear story and Davidson's discovery of the Oregon Caves because he was chasing a bear, a fellow told this one.

It seems a hunter killed a bear in a cave. Naturally, it was pretty dark in there. The hunter crawled into the cave. About the time his eyes adjusted to the darkness, he saw another bear in the cave this one very much alive. We're not sure but we think the bear and the hunter increased the size of the opening to the cave as they both headed out through it at the same time.

—Curry County Echoes. Curry Country Historical Society.
Gold Beach, Ore. Vol. 26. No. 1. January 1998.

Appendix D
The "Christmas" Flood – December 22, 1964

Wind and rain had been heavy for days when on December 22, a collection of downed trees, some up to sixty feet long, as well as general forest debris that had formed a dam and a pond of water, let go resulting in devastation to the Chalet and Chateau which were in the wake of the flood.

The great six-story Chateau suffered damage up to the third floor. At this level, the normally trickling Cave Creek had been purposely routed through enters the building to exit on the first level anf flow on down the canyon.

Because of the storm and flood, the winter crew of just four men and their wives, had been setting up defenses against the time when the avalanche would hit the building. The winter shutters, already up, were checked. Because of the storm, the lodge was without electricity and the telephone line was broken.

About 9:30 on that Tuesday night, the avalanche started down the hill behind the Chalet, across the road from the Chateau, roared under the archway of the Chalet then raced across the driveway and struck the face of the Chateau with full force.

The men, Harry Christensen, the caves manager, Bob Hines, Lee Brown and Gene Bisceglia immediately started breaking the windows and doors to allow the flood to pass through and out the other side.

Lee Brown and Christensen took the latter's wife, who had been injured, out of the building leaving the other three men to face the task of cleanup. The biggest challenge was tons of mud and rock that had swept into the building with the surge of the flood. Wet mud is heavy so steps needed be taken to get the mud and rock out of the building.

At the Chalet, the inundation had taken out three main vertical beams and two horizontal beams that supported the archway. The men's restroom, located at the right of the arch, was beaten to shreds and the gift shop, a few feet away, had lost its doors.

Seventy-five yards away at the Chateau, there was a mass of debris twelve feet thick that totally obliterated the unique lower trout pond and crashed against the wall of the building. It was the mud and rock from this pileup that now devastated the third floor of the building. The quick action of the men in opening a passage by breaking the windows to get the mass to move, saved the generator and furnace.

In the dining room, the decorating of which had just been completed for the anticipated Christmas week crowds, five feet of thick mud and rocks greeted the first inspectors, the three men. French doors that lead out on the causeway had been ripped off. The heavy flow of water had carried light logs out of the building leaving the rocks and mud behind. The supporting pillars had high water marks at the five foot level. About half of the flooring was gone due to the battering of the large logs and rocks – everything crashing to the lower levels. Of the large, elegant staircase, only two steps were left, the remainder having been smashed to kindling and washed out of the building.

Work of relieving the strain on the floor started in the kitchen, where there was three feet of silt. The men, armed with shovels, pushed the mud through a three foot wide hole they cut through the floor. A jury-rigged water system piped water from the River Styx at the cave's entrance to provide drinking water and to flush the floors as the mud was shoveled out. This relief for the floor took the men three dawn-to-dusk days of hard work.

In the meantime, cut off from Cave Junction, the women had salvaged much good food from the storage lockers and used the huge fire place for cooking. In the three weeks of this endeavor the women, among other work, baked 39 loves of bread in a large kettle turned upside down in the fire place for an oven.

Just as some headway was achieved, the storm turned to snow then deposited seven inches on the Monument forcing Hines and Bisceglia to the Chateau's roof with shovels to avoid having the roof collapse. While shoveling the roof, each man twice slipped off the roof but fell into the soft snow below without injury.

Finally, a cat (tractor) forced its way to the lodge from town and cleared much of the outdoor debris from the building, then sandbags were placed around the smashed front of the building to prevent more water from washing into it.

A few days later an electrician arrived to hook up the generator for the auxiliary power plant.

Guest rooms in the Chateau occupy the 4th, 5th and 6th floors and were not touched by the catastrophic flood. But floors 1, 2 and 3 were nearly a total loss.

Two miles below the lodge, the large Lake Creek bridge was so badly damaged that the Caves Highway was closed for weeks while state highway repair crews rebuilt the bridge.

The handful of people who had been at the lodge worked though Christmas Day almost without realizing what day it was. ◇

Dick Rowley, the professional guide who spent most of his life showing visitors the intricacies of the Oregon Caves. He named many of the rooms in the caves.

Appendix E
Names of Caverns, Rooms, and Other Places
On Or Near Oregon Caves National Monument

Dates give year or time-span each name has been known to be used.
Due to the complexity of assembly of names, and the fact that undiscovered
caverns may yet be located and named, this roster cannot be considered complete.
Asterisk (*) indicates contradictory sources. List is Alphabetical.

1st Well - West of Shovel Room in southern end of cave.

Adam's Apple (Old) - Near bridge over the River Styx, 1934 name by Rowley.

Adam's Resting Place - Named by Rowley, 1916. Probably in Adam's Tomb (Macduff, 1917).

Adam's Tomb - Name used by Rowley. This was an old name for the Dry Room (Josephine County Caves, 1915). South of trail's Cathedral Arch. Tours stopped regularly visiting here by the early 1960's. Three white millipedes or centipedes ¾ inch long were seen on broken mud in 1973.

*Agate Rock - East side of East Ghost Room Annex (*Oregon Journal* 1938). A 1934 map places it as the same as Navajo Blankets in the White Formation Passage.

Alligator's Jaw - 1913-1917 - Location unknown, possibly Jaw of Ancient Archetas. Source is photo, possibly taken in Neptune's Grotto Annex.

Angel Falls - Called Bridal Veil Falls from 1916 to at least the 50's.

(The) American Falls - Old name for Niagara Falls. Named by Rowley from 1916 to at least 1924. The current name came into use by 1934.

Arch Angel - A 1916 name by Rowley for Bird of Paradise. Present name first used in 1932.

Arch Hall - Name appears in an article of Sept 3, 1886 in the Grants Pass *Courier*.

Around Cape Horn - *See* Cape Horn.

(The) Atlantic Ocean - Once on the west side of the Rimstone Room. After the color lights were removed in the mid-60's, this name was reassigned to the east side of the room where it remains today. *See* Chesapeake Bay.

Awful Jaws of Death - Same name as Jaws of Death.

Bacon Pantry - In or near the White Formation Passage (Dunham, 1939).

Bacon Room - Layered rock in Paradise Alley area, name by Rowley, 1916.

153

Balcony Room - West of Witherspoon's Hole in southern end of cave. Also known as 2nd well (Knutson, 1975). Just south of the room are openings leading up and to the east along a fault (Knutson (1970).

Banana Grove - Between the 110 Exit and Niagara Falls on the present tour route. Rowley (1916) called it "The Banana Room." A map shows it as "Bananas" (*Oregon Journal*, Apr. 24, 1938). The present name then appeared (Dunham, 1939).

Banana Room. *See* Banana Grove.

Battleship Oregon. *See* Bow of Battleship *Oregon*.

Bear Den's - Natural shallow caves at Exit Tunnel exit. Name in use by 1930.

Bear Pit - Pit across from tree root, 1938-1954.

Beauty's Slide - Unknown cave location, 1891. "The place Mr. Worthington fell was named Beauty's Slide, for the same reason a particularly tall man is nicknamed 'Shorty.'" (Michelson, 1891).

Bee Hive - Mostly likely the same as the Beehive Room (Henthorne, 1913).

Bee Hive Room - First named in 1897.

Beezelbub's Slide - May be same as Devil's Slide, name by Rowley, 1913-1917. It literally means "god of the insects." It may refer to Satan or any devil. In Milton's "Paradise Lost," Beezelbub was Satan's chief lieutenant among the fallen angels.

Bell Chamber - Unknown cave location, 1894.

Belly Crawl - The surveying transit was set on a board somewhere in the cave. (Grants Pass *Bulletin*, July 21, 1930). There were a number of places in the early days where one had to crawl on his belly. Refer to Chapter 2, the 1894 expedition of the San Francisco *Examiner*.

Belthaser - Near bridge over River Styx, name by Rowley, 1934.
It probably refers to Belshazzar, the last king of Babylon. He was warned of defeat by mysterious handwriting that suddenly appeared on a wall.

Big Fir Tree Trail - Name for Big Tree Trail in 1935 (Whitworth).

Big Tree - Discovered in 1923, largest Douglas fir girth in Oregon.

Bird of Paradise. Cave feature that resembled the "Bird of Paradise." This amazing attraction in the cave was stolen in 1996.

Black Slide - A steeply dipping quartz diorite igneous dike at the head of the Stream Passage near Stone's Falls.

Blowhole - 1897 name for Wind Tunnel, called "Zephyr Path" in 1906, "Windy Passage in 1907 and 1915-1916, and Cave of the Winds on 1966 and 1974 maps.

Blue Grotto of Italy - Between Potato Patch and Niagara Falls, just before Snowflake Room, name by Rowley (Dunham, 1939).

154

Bogie Room - Old 1894 name for the South Room. The name derives from the Scottish word for a specter. It also refers to one of the more malicious Little People of Great Britain.

Bone Room - Near western end of cave, west of Witherspoon's Hole and east of Upper Bone Room. Also known as 3rd Well (Knutson, 1975).

(The) Bottomless Pit - Named by Joaquin Miller during Kincaid/Miller/Watson expedition of 1907 (Miller, 1909). Also known as Jacob's Well. 1916 name for area below the stairs leading up and out of the Beehive Room to the 110 Exit. It was used until at least 1955.

Bow of the Battleship *Oregon* - High, sheer wall left and above the light switch for Paradise Lost, as viewed from the Ghost Room Terrace. A 1934 map placed it on a breakdown piece above the Spitting Stone. The Navy's Battleship *Oregon* had the most spectacular history of all U. S. battleships and served in the Spanish-American, First World War and in World War-II. For its colorful duties refer to bibliography for *Battleship Oregon, Bulldog of the Navy.*

Bridal Chamber - Unknown cave location, named in 1897. In 1909 the name was given to a room near the Queen's Palace (*Oregon Observer*, Sept. 12, 1909). It lay somewhere between the 110 Exit and the Wind Tunnel (Josephine County Caves, 1915). From 1916 to 1924 (at least) it was the name for the Wedding Cake Room. Joaquin Miller's Chapel was labeled the Bridal Chamber in a 1930's-? photo. In 1966 the "Wedding Cake" appeared on a map.

Bridal Room - Unknown cave location, named in 1894.

Bridal Veil Falls - Name for Angel Falls from 1916 to at least the 1950's.

Bride - In Passageway of the White Formation, name by Rowley, 1916.

Bowery - Unknown location, name by Rowley, 1913-1917.

The Bride - Name for formation in Wedding Cake Room from 1916 to the present. In 1966 the "Wedding Cake" appeared on a map.

Bulkhead - Carbide Room Wall on 1934 map.

Burned Forest - Unknown cave location (*Oregon Journal*, 1917).

Bush Lake - In or near Royal Gorge (Rowley, 1917).

Butterfly - Near the Bacon Pantry in the White Formation Passage (Dunham, 1939) *See also* Cave Butterfly, Onyx Butterfly.

Caesar's Column - District Forester's (1917) name for Grand Column.

Camp Henderson - A cabin located on Sucker Creek. It was used as a rest area on the trail from Williams to the caves in the early 1900's. It was probably built by the Oregon Caves Improvement Company in the late 1880's.

Canadian Falls - *See* Old Niagara Falls.

Candy Room - Unknown cave location, name by Rowley, 1913-1917.

Canyon Passage - Split into Northern and Southern Canyon Passages by the construction of the Exit Tunnel.

Cape Horn ("Growing around Cape Horn") - Apparently a tight squeeze near today's Adam's Tomb, name by Rowley, 1917 to 1924.

Cape Horn Map - Unknown cave location. It apparently referred to a relief map that showed the nearby Strait of Magellan (Romer, 1926).

Carbide Room - Northwest annex of Watson's Grotto.

Cascades - 1916 and 1917 Rowley's name for flowstone to the right of the upper metal stairs to Bird of Paradise (west of telephone). Also called Cascade.

Catawampus - Between Watson's Grotto and the Devil's Backbone. It is sometimes called Gatawampus or One-eyed Gatawampus, a mythical monster of the north woods.

Cathedral Arch - "Vaulted ceiling above tour route at the 110 Exit. Named first in 1934 by Rowley.

Cathedral Chamber - Unknown cave location, 1894. Visiting reporters from San Francisco *Examiner* made musical notes by banging on formations. Chapter 2. *See* Musical Stalactites

Cathedral Chimes - Near 110 Exit in Cathedral Arch, name by Rowley, 1916 and 1920.

Cave Alligator - A Speleogen projecting out over the river 3 feet south of the east end of the bridge was called "The Jawbone of the Ancient Archetas" or "The Jawbone" by Rowley from 1916 through the mid-1920's.

Cave Butterfly - Near the Bacon Pantry in or near the White Formation Passage, also called Butterfly and Onyx Butterfly (Dunham, 1939).

Cave Camel - Called "Kneeling Camel" in 1916-1917, Imagination Room.

Cave Creek - Name dates from 1913 (Rowley) and is the present name for the stream after it exits Oregon Caves until it empties into Sucker Creek. The surface stream above the cave is sometimes called Upper Cave Creek before it disappears into the ground – under ground it is called the River Styx. After emerging, the water runs through a culvert and into the trout pool in front of The Chateau. The creek resumes on the opposite side of the small pool then runs through the third floor Dining Room of the lodge then out under the ground floor of the six story building, and down the ravine.

Cave Mountain - *See* Mount Elijah.

Cave of the Winds - Trail between Joaquin Miller's Chapel and Grand Column.

Caveman - In Kudgel's Cave, Rowley's name.

Caveman's Fool - Paradise Lost Platform.

Chamber of the Dead - Above? the Suspended Ceiling near the Ghost Room (Dunham, 1939).

Chamber of Mystery - 20 foot by 30 foot chamber located 30 feet above Watson's Grotto and 40 feet below the Imagination Room, named by an 1888 tourist.

Chesapeake Bay - The name for the old Atlantic Ocean, 1923-1954. However, both names have been mentioned together (*Oregon Journal*, July 1, 1923).

Chief Rain-in-the-Face - Old name for formation in high area of Royal Gorge. Same as Rain-in-the-Face (Macduff, 1917). It was "a monument dedicated to Joaquin Miller" (*Oregon Journal*, July 1, 1923).

Chicken Graveyard - Old name for Faucet Room off Wind Tunnel. On maps marked 1934, 1938, 1966 (*Oregon Journal*).

Christmas Tree - Recent name for stalagmite on south wall of Ghost Room.

Climax - One of the Two Little Owls near Jacob's Well. The other one was called Max (Dunham, 1939).

Clobberstone - Recent name for low lying ceiling rock above Imagination Room Stairs. Also called Scatterbrains as what supposedly might happen to those without hard hats.

Coke Bottle - Recent name for hourglass-like formation in lower part of Imagination Room.

Cookie Monster - Recent name for Jaws of Death. See also Slime Monster.

Coral Chamber - Perhaps the same as the Coral Gardens, name by Rowley, 1913-1917.

Coral Garden(s) - SW parallel to, below and to left of Banana Grove. 1916 to present, name by Rowley.

Crater Lake - East of Wind Tunnel, 1916 to present, name by Rowley.

Crawlway Complex - East of North Ghost Room Annex (Knutson, 1975). 750 feet long surveyed in 1971.

Crystal Club Room - West of North Ghost Room Annex and above Miller's Chapel and Golden Stairs. 223 feet long surveyed in 1971. The small crystals at the end of the stalactites indicate very humid conditions.

Crystal Lake - In Passageway of the White Formation, name by Rowley, 1916.

Cudjo's Cave - 1954 name for North Ghost Room Annex.

Cupid's Room - NW extension of Queen's Reception Room, 1966 to present.

Dan Cupid - Unknown cave location, a formation (Saunders, 1924).

Dance Hall - A Mazama Club trip described the "Dance Hall with its wonderful floor made by nature for the fairy folk." (Grants Pass *Courier*, 1922).

Dante's Inferno - Old name for the Stream Grotto, the lower part of the Ghost Room (Horner, 1919), 1916-mid 1960's Rowley's name for lowest part of the Ghost Room by the River Styx. Romer (1924) used it as a synonym for the Ghost Chamber. Red and blue lights were used there from the early 1930's to the mid-1960's turning the view into a Hollywood showplace. Dante Alighleri (1265-1321) wrote a fictional account about the nature of the Christian hell.

Davidson's Bear Pit - Pit across tree root by Kincaid/Miller/Watson expedition of 1907 (Miller, 1909). By Rowley 1917.

Dead Sea - Unknown cave location, name by Rowley, 1913-1917.

Devil's Backbone - Named by editor of Grants Pass *Courier* in 1886 as "a sharp rock with deep caverns on either side" and in 1888 by a tourist, a steep "ridge." Formerly in old tour connection between Watson's Grotto and the Imagination Room. Now known as Roosevelt's Ride. Removal of the Devil's Backbone was begun by the CCC in 1935; it is now largely destroyed. Refer to Joaquin Miller's description of it from his 1909 visit in Chapter 7. Also known as Roosevelt's Rough Ride (Meyers, 1907), Teddy's Rough Ride (Rowley, 1913-1917) and Satan's Backbone.

Devil's Banquet Hall - 1889 (Steel) to 1895 (Mitchell) name for Ghost Room.

Devil's Bear Pit - Across from Tree Root, named by Rowley.

Devil's Cauldron - 1914 name for area below and south of bridge over the River Styx.

Devil's Chamber - Queen's Reception Room. Labeled in 1913 photo and in brochure (Josephine County Caves, 1915).

Devil's Cradle - Probably first named by Rowley, name still in use in 1954. Speleogen directly above east end of the bridge over the River Styx.

Devil's Dance Hall - Perhaps same as Ghost Room, name by Rowley, 1913-1917. Also called Dance Hall (1913).

Devil's Gap - 1888 name for a point along the passageway to the Imagination Room, may also have been called Jack Passage.

Devil's Pass - Wind Tunnel, named by Walter C. Burch on 1885 trip. *See* Appendix B.

Devil's Pit - Named by editor of Grants Pass *Courier* in 1886 as the editor toured the caves. In 1888 name for Jacob's Well.

Devil's Potato Patch - First used by Dunham (1939). Probably name for same area as Potato Patch.

Devil's Punchbowl - 1 foot wide Rimstone pool at eye level near top of where old ladder used to come up from bottom of the Imagination Room, on the SE wall along the ledge. First named by Rowley in 1916. Called Little Mirror Lake in 1934. Mirror Lake had to be filled up every day sometime between 1937-1941 (Keizer, 1977).

Devil's Slide - Below Rimstone Room. Name from Rowley, 1916 to present. Visited by Rowley's tours.

Devil's Stairway - Near Rimstone Room, name by Rowley, 1913-1917.

Devil's Washboard - The east side of the Rimstone Room from 1916 to the mid-1960's. In 1932, red lights were placed there until the mid-1960's, when the name and the lights were eliminated.

Deveraux's Hole - Eastern end of South Room.

Diamond Hall - Paradise Alley Extension. Named by Burch (1887) during 1885 trip. After squeezing through Hell's Gate, Burch entered a small chamber, went down a 12 foot hole and came to the hall which Burch said was 184 feet from the cave's entrance. *See* Appendix B. There was "a crystal pool 8 feet deep."

Dining Hall - 1891 and 1897 name, possibly name for Ghost Room.

Dining Room - Above 110 Exit, 1891.

Dolly Parton - More recent name for earlier actress Mae West.

The Dome - Unknown cave location, 1902 and 1913, probably Paradise Lost.

Dome Complex - Leads upward from south end of cave. Discovered and at least partly mapped in 1962. Snail shells indicate a connection with the surface.

Dragon's Den - In Paradise Alley - Wind Tunnel, name from Rowley, 1917.

Dragon's Mouth - Unknown cave location, from 1924 photo.

Drapery Room - Niagara Falls, 1902 and 1913.

The Drawing Room - 1906 and 1915 name for Rimstone Room as the scalloped floor looked like a rich carpet (Josephine County Caves, 1915).

Dry Room - Old name was Adam's Tomb (Josephine County Caves, 1915).

Duck Tail - Recent name in Imagination Room.

Dulcimer Hall - Paradise Alley, named in 1888.

Eagle Room - 1894 name for Neptune's Grotto *which see.*

Ear of Corn Room - 1897 name for Adam's Tomb.

East Ghost Room Annex - East of Paradise Lost.

Echo Dome - South of Balcony Room.

Eel - Recent name in Imagination Room.

Eiffel Tower - Unknown cave location (*Oregon Journal,* 1917).

Elephant Chamber - Name appears in an article of Sept 3, 1886 in the Grants Pass *Courier.* Refer to Appendix B. *See* Elephant's Head.

Elephant's Head - Near Wind Tunnel and after Paradise Alley, name from Rowley, 1916-1917.

Elfin Jail - Near Niagara Falls, name from Rowley, had algae growing in front of it (Dunham, 1939).

Elijah's Bear - Recent name in Imagination Room.

Elijah Davidson's Statue - Near Wind Tunnel, name from Rowley, 1916.

Elijah's Cave - First known name of Oregon Caves, used by Wm. W. Fiddler in his article in *Morning Oregonian* Aug. 1, 1877. See Chapter 1.

Elijah's Entrance - District Forester's (1917) name for Lower Entrance.

ET - Recent name in Imagination Room.

Excellent Room - Located through tight crawlway on right side of Wedding Cake Room. Contains longest known soda straw in cave (18 inches).

Exit Tunnel Cave - Near end of Exit Tunnel.

Fairy Bower - Unknown cave location, 1906.

Fairy Dance Hall - 1934 Name for left side of the passage leading from the Throne Room to Neptune's Grotto.

Fairy Garden - Near Petrified Forest, named by Rowley (Dunham, 1939).

Fat Lady's Squeeze - Rowley's name. Trail end of room, now called "Squeeze" or "The Squeeze."

Fat Man's Grief - Just past the Wishing Post, was thus named from 1916 to about 1924.

Fat Man's Misery - 1934 name for steps between the Beehive Room and 110 Exit.

Fat Women's Misery - Unknown cave location, named in 1897 by Acklen.

Filled with Rock and Dirt - A map name for Shovel Room in the southern part of the cave.

First Well - North of Small Dome in southern part of cave.

Floral Chamber - Unknown cave location, 1906.

Floral Hall - 1897 name for Paradise Lost.

Flower Vase in Miniature - Perhaps between Petrified Gardens and Joaquin Miller's Chapel (*Oregon Journal*, July 1,1923).

Fountain of Everlasting Youth - Probably originally the Fountain of Tyreen.

Fountain of Tyreen - Leaving Lake Michigan - "where Joaquin Miller always watered his enchanted horse" (Rowley, 1934). This probably became known as the "Fountain of Everlasting Youth." (Dunham, 1939).

Fourth Well - Near Upper Bone Room (Knutson, 1975). Contains a rodent's nest.

Frozen River of Alaska - In Passageway of the White Formation, name by Rowley, 1916. Also known as Frozen River (Macduff, 1917).

*Garden of Eden - In Ghost Room, name by Rowley, 1913-1917, possibly Rain Room. A 1934 map places it in the annex southeast of the Paradise Lost ladder.

Garden of the Gods - Shelf-like balcony above Lake Michigan in Joaquin Miller's Chapel, Name 1916 to present.

Gatawampus - *See* Catawampus.

Generator Room - 1934 map name for Transformer Room. Small alcove northeast of the 110 Exit.

George Washington - A "circular tower 6 feet in diameter and 50 feet high, in the Toy Room (Nickerson, 1914).

George Washington's Statue - Located in the Ghost Room, named in 1897 by Acklen.

George and Martha Washington - White stalagmites on south wall seen from Angel Falls Platform in the Ghost Room. George has "tight pants" and Martha has a "hoop skirt."

Ghost Chamber - Original name for Joaquin Miller's Chapel, named by Burch on 1885 trip. A 1902 photo labels the Chapel as the Ghost Chamber. Joaquim Miller lists it as a place he visited during Kincaid/Miller/Watson expedition of 1907 (Miller, 1909). It was a common name for the Chapel from 1894 to 1914, on account of two white columns which Burch discovered. *See* Appendix C. At least part of it was formerly called Dante's Inferno (Horner, 1919).

Ghost Room Upper Level - 4,135 feet long of surveyed passage.

Giant's Tongue - Unknown cave location, 1891.

Gilmore - Formation resembling African lion, right of stairs into Rimstone Room. (The name "Gilmore" appears to refer to the drawing of a roaring lion use in promoting "Roar With Gilmore Blue-Green Gasoline' in 1920's-1930's.)

Glacier Rock - Rock under ladder at back of Kincaid's Dance Hall, name by Rowley, 1913-1917.

*Golden Stairs - Between North Ghost Room Annex and Crystal Club Room. May be along fault. Exiting Wedding Cake Room to Bird of Paradise. Name 1906 to present (Henthorne, 1913). 179' feet long surveyed in 1971.

Golden Stairway - On "third floor," Named by Miller during Kincaid/Miller /Watson expedition of 1907 (Miller, 1909). Probably the same as the Golden Stairs.

Gopher - Recent name in Imagination Room.

Grand Canyon of the Colorado - 1934 Rowley's name for lower area south of Angel Falls. A 1934 map called it Grand Canyon.

Grand Column - Between Neptune's Grotto and Wind Tunnel on visitor trail. 1,053 feet from Entrance, 70 feet higher, 95 feet below surface. Called "Pillar Room" from 1914 to 1916. Rowley called it "Caesar's Column" and Grand Column (its present name) in 1917.

Grandma's (Tea) Kettle - In Paradise Alley, name by Rowley, 1916.

Graveyard - Unknown cave location, named in 1897. Name in 1916 (Rowley) for northeast annex of Chapel. Second largest room in cave (Horner, 1919, Nickerson, 1914)), 75 feet long and 25 feet wide. Bones found here by Rowley in 1922. The latter locations may be Paradise Alley.

Graveyard - SE part of Ghost room, named from 1914 to mid-1930's.

Graveyard Scene - Unknown cave location (*Oregon Journal*, 1917).

Great Dinosaur - Unknown cave location.

Great Ghost Room - Name for Ghost Room (Dunham, 1939).

Great Gosh-What-Is-It? - Unknown cave location. Resembled the jaws of some creature (Laing, 1917).

Great Limestone Caves - Second known name (1886) of Oregon Cave.

Great Oregon Caves - Third known name of Oregon Cave, used by Weister.

Great Suspended Ceiling - 1934 name for ceiling of South Ghost Room Annex.

(The) Grotto - East side of Joaquin Miller's Chapel, 1915. A 1934 map placed it in the River Styx Annex to the Ghost Room.

Guardian of the Cave - Unknown location but may be near the 110 Exit. Attributed to Michelson, 1891. *See* Chapter 3.

Hanging Gardens of Babylon - Name for King and Queen's Throne Room from 1939 to at least 1956 (Matthew, 1965).

Headhunter's Trophy Room - A little alcove right (west) side of the tour path as one leaves the Ghost Room. Rowley named it starting in 1939. Also called "The Squirrel's Cage."

Heart of Old Chief Rain in the Face - Above Wigwam.

Heavenly Boudoir - Western Annex of Petrified Gardens, 1909-1924.

*Hell's Gate - A crawlway from King and Queen's Throne Room to Neptune's Grotto, name by Walter C. Burch on August 6, 1884. It started immediately after the King and Queen's Throne room on the present tour. Burch enlarged the hole with small shots of powder in 1885. *See* Appendix B.

Holy of Holies - On "third floor." Named by Miller during the Kincaid/ Miller/ Watson expedition of 1907 (Miller, 1909). Near Ghost Room, name used by Rowley, 1913-1917.

Honeycomb - Recent name in Imagination Room.

Hornet's Nest. Name appears in an article of Sept 3, 1886 in the Grants Pass *Courier.*

Horsetail Falls - Old name for the Wedding Cake (*Oregon Journal*, 1938). Named for a falls in the Columbia Gorge.

Imagination Room - Original name was Wigwam.

Inside-out Gopher Hole - Called Ostrich Head in 1916-1917.

Jewel Casket - Unknown cave location (*Oregon Journal*, 1917).

Joaquin Miller's Chapel - Rowley name (1916) for northeast annex of Chapel.

Jack Passage - *See* Devil's Gap .

Jacob's Well - Pit in Dry Room that descends to Adam's Tomb. The pit under the Paradise Lost stairs has also been called "Jacob's Well."

Jailhouse - On right, before Niagara Falls, 1954, or on Niagara Falls, 1966.

Jawbone (of the Ancient Archetas) - A Speleogen projecting out over the River Styx three feet south of the east end of the bridge was called this name by Rowley from 1916 through the mid-1920's.

Jaws of Death - Below Mother Owl and near Jacob's Well (Dunham, 1939).

Jefferson Meyers' Room - Named by Miller during Kincaid/Miller/Watson expedition of 1907 (Miller, 1909). Name for Ghost Room area, 1907-1920.

Joaquin Miller's Chapel - Name by Rowley for room between Wind Tunnel and Rimstone Room. An article by Joaquin Miller in Southern Pacific Railroad's magazine *Sunset* in 1909, gave the cave wide publicity on the west coast and helped increase visitation and the demand for the creation of the monument.

Joaquin Miller's Room - Name for Chapel 1907 (Watson, 1909).

Joaquin's Rest - Unknown cave location in 1907 (Watson, 1909).

Joseph's Tomb - "First floor," named by Miller during Kincaid/Miller/Watson expedition of 1907 (Miller, 1909), used by Rowley, 1913-1917.

Josephine County - Named for Lloyd Rollins' daughter, Josephine, perhaps the first white woman to live in the area. It is the only county in Oregon to be named after a woman.

Josephine County Caves - Sixth name (1915) for Oregon Caves.

Although Dick Rowley was a no non-nonsense guide, he is reported to have been able to tell some wild stories about the caves to thrill his guests. When on duty, which was most of the time, he wore mid-calf boots and always a hat.

Judge - District Forester's (1917) name for formation in Judicial Hall.

Judicial Hall - Near Beehive, at end of Royal Gorge, 1916-1924.

Jules Verne's Well - South of Junction Room. Water enters River Styx (Sims) - Visited by Rowley's tours. Name from 1894 to the present time. First used by San Francisco *Examiner* exploration expedition. (*See* Chapter 2) Plausible the name may refer to two different areas.

Junction Room - East of North Ghost Room Annex and above Jules Verne's Well (Knutson, 1975). About 20 feet high and 15 feet across. It contains flowstone, dripstone and crystal lined pools. At the junction with the Ghost Room is a vertical quartz diorite igneous dike about 6 inches wide.

Jury - District Forester's (1917) name for formation in Judicial Hall.

Kansas Tornado in Wheatfield - Recent name in Imagination Room.

Katzenjammer Kids - Named for two characters in a comic strip of the 1920's-30's by that title. Perhaps in Imagination Room. (Saunders, 1924).

Kincaid's Dance Hall - Named by Joaquin Miller during Kincaid/Miller/Watson expedition of 1907 (Miller, 1909). Was name for South Ghost Room Annex until present day except for mid-1960's.

King Nebuchadnezzar - *See* Old King Nebuchadnezzar.

King Solomon's Mines - Named by Steel (1889) during 1888 trip, possibly the Imagination Room or at least near the 110 Exit.

King's Chamber - Upper caves, 1914.

King's Hall - Unknown cave location in 1907 (Watson, 1909). It lay somewhere between the 110 Exit and Wind Tunnel (Josephine County Caves, 1915).

King's Hallway - Unknown cave location, 1906-1915.

King's Highway - Probably Paradise Alley, name by Miller during Kincaid/Miller/Watson expedition of 1907 (Miller, 1909). Rowley, 1913-1917.

King's Palace - The King and Queen's Throne Room, since at least 1916 (possibly 1917) up until the late 1960's, was called the "Kings Palace." Was named by Miller during Kincaid/Miller/Watson expedition of 1907 (Miller, 1909), or "Kings Throne Room." The name was used by Fidler (1919) in an 1877 trip (*See* Chapter 1) to refer to a formation-rich room close to the main entrance, possibly Petrified Gardens.

King's Wine Cellar - Located in King's Palace (*Oregon Journal*, 1938) Leading off from the top of the Petrified Forest Room is a low crawlway which proceeds to this low chamber. A 1975 map locates this as a basement room out of the Dry Room/Grand Column passages.

Kneeling Camel - Imagination Room (Macduff, 1917) or between Adam's Tomb and Jacob's Well.

Kudgel's Cave - Rowley's name for North Ghost Room Annex, the room between the Rimstone Room and the Ghost Room Terrace.

Lake Michigan - Small pool south of Mt. Shasta. Regular tour visits here stopped about 1931.

Lamb's Head - Recent name for area above Slime Monster.

Large Room Filled with Rock - A map label for the South Room.

Last Chance Chamber - Named by editor of Grants Pass *Courier* in essay published Sept. 3, 1886. *See* Appendix C. In 1888 name for Beehive Room, changed to present name in 1913. The name comes from flowstone that looks like a great hornet's nest. *See* Hornets Nest.

Last Natural Room - Name on map by at least 1972.

Lion's Jaw - Unknown cave location, named in 1897. Near Banana Grove, 1911-1917, named by Rowley in 1916.

Lion's Head - Unknown cave location (*Oregon Journal*, 1917).

Little Bush Lake - In Imagination Room, past Catawampus and before Prison Cells on 1915 tour.

Little Grayback Creek - Older name for Sucker Creek.

Little Mammoth - 1888 name for Imagination Room, later called Wigwam from 1923-1975.

Little Mirror Lake - 1934 name for Devil's Punchbowl.

(Little) Mount(ain) Pit - Unknown location, named by Rowley (1916). Possibly near Dry Room, 1916-1924.

Little Prison Cell - Near Niagara Falls.

Little Shepherd Boy - Broken stalagmite leaving Niagara.

Little Teddy Bear - Above Mary's Little Lamb.

The Living Glacier - Possibly flowstone near (south of) Angel Falls, by Rowley, 1934.

Logan Creek - 1888 name for Cave Creek from mouth of cave to confluence with Sucker Creek. Name changed to Cave Creek in 1913.

Lost Cord - Located in lower part of cave, refers to string leading out of cave to prevent being lost having been lost, 1891. *See* Chapter 3.

Lotus - King Neptune's daughter, a column in Neptune's Grotto.

Lower Stream Passage - During high flow has only 1/3 flow of River Styx at main entrance (Knutson, 1970). It usually becomes a trickle during the end of the summer.

Madonna - Near Exit Tunnel (Dunham, 1939).

Mae West - Twin stalagmites near entrance to King and Queen's Throne Room. A more recent name is Dolly Parton. *See also* Dolly Parton.

Maid's Parlor - Mentioned in Grants Pass *Courier* in 1886. Between 110 Exit and Hell's Gate.

Mammoth Chamber - 1885 to 1888 name for Ghost Room, first named by Burch on his 1884 exploratory trip. *See* Appendix B.

Mammoth Column - Name seems to have been applied to Grand Column by a photographer (Patterson) in 1923. (*See* picture page 74, and Appendix B)

Managerie Hall - The Wedding Cake Room, name by Rowley, 1917-1934.

Marble Halls of Oregon - Fourth known name (1907) for Oregon Cave, used by

Joaquin Miller in 1909 article about a 1907 trip.

Marty Clark Dome - Above junction of Wind Tunnel and Joaquin Miller Chapel (Knutson, 1975). Named after a signature found there in 1971.

Mary's Little Lamb - In Imagination Room, name by Rowley, 1913-1917.

Max - One of the Two Little Owls near Jacob's Well. Also called Maxine. The other baby owl was called Climax (Dunham, 1939).

Mile Canyon - May be the same as Grand Canyon of the Colorado (Dunham, 1939).

Mirror Room - Water pools in lower part of cave, named by first *Examiner* party in 1891.

Monte Cristo's Treasure Chamber - Named in 1894 by 2nd *Examiner* expedition – see artist's sketch on page 53. Possibly in Wedding Cake Room. Edmond Dante was the hero of The Count of Monte Cristo, by Alexandre Dumas. Dante's is sentenced on a false charge to life imprisonment in the Chateau d'If. After many years, with the help of a fellow inmate who had laboriously dug through thick walls, he manages to escape. He finds buried treasure in a cave on the island of Monte Cristo, the whereabouts of which he has learned in prison, and becomes a powerful and vengeful figure.

Moonmilk Area - Name 1966 to present. Small complex of passages located to the south of the main entrance and is entered via either of two passages which lead west from the Shortcut Passage near the point where it passes beneath the Wigwam Room. 226 feet surveyed in 1971. A bulkhead in this area prevents access to the surface. At least one passage is very close to the surface.

Moses' Chamber - Possibly old name for Dry Room, named by Rowley, 1913-1917. Also used by Miller during the Kincaid/Miller/Watson expedition of 1907 (Miller, 1909) for an unidentified room on the "first floor."

Mother Owl - Near Jacob's Well and her Two Little Owls, Max, and Climax (Dunham, 1939).

Mount Elijah - Named in 1931. Mt. Elijah has an elevation of 6,390 feet (*See* Grayback Mountain topo). Is about half a mile southwest of Lake Peak (6,642 ft. elev.). The Oregon Caves are under Mt. Elijah's northwestern slopes at the 4,000 foot elevation. The name Mount Elijah was adopted by the United States Board of Geographic Names (USBGN) in 1930-1931 in honor of Elijah J. Davidson, who discovered the caves in 1874. Old names were Oregon Caves Mountain, Mount Sand and Cave Mountain but these names were never well established. (Reference: *Oregon Geographic Names* Sixth Ed. and *Geographic Names Information System – Oregon* U. S. Geological Survey)

Mount Hood Chamber - Old name for Mt. Shasta Room, named in 1888.

Mount Sand - *See* Mount Elijah.

Mt. Pitt - Between Beehive Room and Adam's Tomb on old tour route (Macduff, 1917). (Mt. Pitt is an old but still popular name for Mount McLoughlin near Crater Lake and was named for the "Pit Indians" (Modoc and Klamath) who built pits in which to trap game. The name Mt. McLoughlin was established on a map in 1838, first called Mt. Pitt in 1843. But the Oregon Legislature restored the McLoughlin name in 1905, which was approved by the U.S. Board of Geological Names (USBGN) in 1912. For an exceptional photograph of Mt. McLoughlin see the book *Oregon's Names; How to Say Them and Where Are They Located* p.70.

(Old) Mount Shasta - Stalagmite in Joaquin Miller's Chapel. Name from 1917 to present. Was probably called Mt. Hood in 1888.

Multnomah Falls - 1934 Rowley's name for The Cascades.

Muppet Balcony - Recent name in Imagination Room.

Music Room - Near Beehive, 1913-24. Once called Musical Room.

Musical Room - Old name for Music Room.

Musical Stalactites - *See* Cathedral Chamber. For description see age 56.

Naked Lady - Below the Bone Dome Entrance.

Navajo Blanket(s) - Cave bacon drapery, in Passageway of the White Formation, name by Rowley, 1916.

Neptune's Grotto - First named by Rowley in 1916. Between Petrified Forest and Banana Grove on the trail. Obsolete name may have been Orchestra Gallery. Original name was Eagle Room (1894).

Neptune's Daughter - Just off the floor, below a flowstone "canopy" in NW part of Neptune's Grotto. Pointed out from 1920 to at least 1954. The supposed bare back of Neptune's shy daughter while she was bathing.

New Dome - In Ghost Room above Paradise Lost (Knutson, 1975).

Niagara Falls - Between Petrified Forest and Banana Grove on trail. Named by Joaquin Miller during Kincaid/Miller/Watson expedition of 1907 (Miller, 1909). Also called American Falls.

(Old) Niagara Falls - Also called the Old Niagara Falls and Canadian Falls. It is in Paradise Alley eâst of Crater Lake and the Wind Tunnel. From 1907 to 1924 the only formation called Niagara Falls in the cave. Gours in the room above. NW in an upper passage leading to Crater Lake is a large rodent incisor.

(Old) Nick's Bedroom (or chamber) - Passage over and south of Banana Grove. Name from 1894 to present. Also called Nick's Bedchamber (Miller, during Kincaid/Miller/Watson expedition of 1907 (Miller, 1909), and Old Nick's Bed-room. Old Nick's Bedroom was also a name for a room close to the lower entrance (Grants Pass *Courier*, 1935).

Nick's Slide - Named by Joaquim Miller during Kincaid/Miller/Watson expedition of 1907 (Miller, 1909). The old name for Devil's Slide. On either side is the Bottomless Pit *which see*.

Nick's Toboggan - Breakdown in Paradise Alley, name by Rowley, 1916-1917. Same as Old Satan's Toboggan Ride.

Nieland's Passage - Extends north from spiral stairs, near Queen's Dining Room.

No Name Creek - Named by 1934. One of its headwaters begins in the Monument.

North Canyon Passage - North of Exit Tunnel jog.

North Canyon Passage Extension - Continues to the east (Knutson, 1975).

North Country - In or near White Formation Passage (Dunham, 1939).

North Ghost Room Annex - Area above the Rimstone Room. It connects Miller's Chapel with the Ghost Room.

Old Bear Pens - Area near where concession garage now stands.

Old Charon - Formation somewhere near the Bridge Over the River Styx. (Dunham, 1939). Charon was the Greek spirit who ferried people across the River Styx to the land of the dead.

Old Hag - Recent name in Imagination Room.

Old King Nebuchadnezzar of the Jews - Also called King Nebuchadnezzar. Found in the Bible in Jeremiah 39:1. Stalagmite is down and to the left in his hanging gardens in the King and Queen's Throne Room.

Old Man of the Mountain - Recent name in Imagination Room, probably Chief-Rain-in-the-Face.

Old Mount Shasta - See Mount Shasta.

Old Nick's Punchbowl - May be same as Devil's Punchbowl *which see*, named by McDuff (1917).

Old Satan's Cauldron - Named by Joaquin Miller (1909) for pit in Petrified Gardens. Rowley's 1916 and 1924 name for Devil's Cauldron, lower area below and south of the Bridge Over the River Styx.

Old Satan's Cradle - 1916-1920's name for upward projecting rock on a ledge directly above the east end of the Bridge Over the River Styx.

Old Satan's Face and Eyes - In Paradise Alley, name by Rowley, 1916-1917.

(Old) Satan's Hitching Post - Plausibly same as Old Hitching Post.

Old Satan's Slide - 1907-1924 name for Devil's Slide.

Old Satan's Toboggan Ride - Same as Nick's Toboggan *which see*.

(Old) Scalp Rock - *See* Scalp Rock.

The (Old) Wishing Post - First so named in 1934, was called ("Old) Satan's Hitching Post" from 1916 to the mid-1920's.

One Eyed Gatawampus - Same as Catawampus.

Onyx Butterfly - In White Formation Passage, 1934. It was also called The Butterfly or simply Butterfly (Dunham, 1939).

Onyx Castle - In White Formation Passage, named in 1934 (*Oregon Journal*, 1938).

Orchestra Gallery - Possibly Neptune's Grotto, 1906 (*Observer*, [Grants Pass] 1912)

Oregon Caves - Fifth known name for Oregon Cave, used in 1909 presidential proclamation creating the monument. (*See* Page 1 of this book.) Also used by the Oregon Conservation Commission in 1911.

Oregon Cave - Last name used for Oregon Cave. Use started in the early 1900's when it was realized that the two entrances were part of the same cave.

Oregon Caves Mountain - *See* Mount Elijah.

Oregon Grape - Between Squeeze and Beehive (Dunham, 1939).

Oregon Loft - Paradise Lost. Named in 1894, used by Miller (1909) and by Rowley, 1913-1917.

Oregon Mammoth Cave - Name for Oregon Cave used by the Portland mountaineering club, the Mazamas, which visited it in mass in 1913.

Organ Loft - Somewhere near Joaquin Miller's Chapel, 1894, 1913. "Tall rows of columns stood in regular array like the pipes of an immense organ." (Henthorne, 1913)

Ostrich Head - Between Beehive Room and Adam's Tomb. Macduff, 1917. Name used by Rowley (1916) for unidentified formation.

Owls - Probably the same as The Two Little Owls.

Owl's Nest - Platform under Paradise Lost on south side, 1913.

Pacific Ocean - The west side became the "Pacific Ocean" in the mid-1960's in the Rimstone Room.

The Palace - Past 110 Exit, 1914.

Paradise Alley - The southern continuation of the passage which contains the Grand Column. It ends at Crater Lake. Rodent and/or bat bones occur at the south end. Visited by Rowley's tours. Named by Dick Rowley (1916). 365 feet long surveyed in 1971.

Paradise Alley Extension - East of Niagara Falls.

Paradise Lost - Named first in 1897. From 1906 to 1915 this name was used for a room near the Imagination Room and before the 110 Exit, or for an area after the Banana Grove on the tour. (Grants Pass *Courier*, 1935).

Visited by poet Joaquin Miller in 1907 who defined the site as a "creepy place" (Miller, 1909) – *See* chapter 3."

Paradise Lost Dome - East end of Ghost Room.

Passageway of the Whale - 350 feet from Entrance, 59 feet higher, 70 feet below surface, between Bridge Over the River Styx and Dry Room. Name in use since 1934.

Paul Bunyan - Rowley's name for formation in Imagination Room.

Petrified Forest - Named since 1909 by Rowley. Near Neptune's Grotto.

Petrified Garden - Named since 1916, 203 feet from Entrance, 12 feet higher, 55 feet below surface. Between Watson's Grotto and Bridge Over the River Styx.

Pigeons Roost - Near Center of Ghost Room on ceiling.

Pillar Room - Second floor. Named during Kincaid/Miller/Watson expedition of 1907 (Miller, 1909). Name from 1914 to 1916 for the room called The Grand Column. Rowley called the formation "Caesar's Column" and Grand Column in 1917.

Pipe Organ - In Paradise Alley, name by Rowley, 1913-1917. *See* White House.

The Pit - Unknown cave location, 1913.

Poltergeist - Recent name in Imagination Room.

Potato Patch - Name first used in 1966 guide manual, probably same formations as Devil's Potato Patch.

President's Room - 1906 and 1915 name for Ghost Room.

Prehistoric Pool - Between 110 Exit and Banana Grove. There was supposed to be what looked like an ancient hippopotamus rising from the pool (Dunham, 1939).

Pride of Oregon - (1914-1917) name for Paradise Lost or its formations (Macduff, 1917). From 1906 to 1915 the present name was used for a room near the Imagination Room and before the 110 Exit.

Pride of the Caves - Mammoth drapery in Paradise Lost. Named in 1915 (Josephine County Caves).

Princess' Bedroom - Named on a 1938 and 1966 map. Shelf on SW side of Cupid's Room. Antechamber to Queen's Reception Room.

Prison Cell(s) - Royal Gorge Entrance, near Imagination Room and Before Niagara Falls, named by Rowley, 1916-1917, 1934.

Pulpit - Washington's Monument, 1915. Named in 1915 (Josephine County Caves).

Queen's Apartments - Unknown cave location, 1902 photo.

*Queen's Cellar - Between 110 Exit and Hell's Gate, named in 1885. May have been original name for King and Queen's Throne Room used by Burch on 1885 cave trip. Mentioned in Grants Pass *Courier* 1886. *See* Appendix B.

Queen's Chamber - Unknown cave location, 1909-1915.

Queen's Dining Room - Name by Rowley (1916) still in use. A low opening beneath the steel stairs on the east side of the passage opening into the room leads to a blocked passage just north of the Grand Column.

Queen Josephine's Place of Abode - Near Coral Gardens, name by Rowley, 1920. Josephine de Beauharnais (1763-1814) was the empress of France and the first wife of Napoleon.

Queen's Organ - Stalactites hit in Joaquin Miller's Chapel to produce musical sound. Maybe different location from Cathedral Chamber "Musical Stalactites *which see.* Refer to Chapter 2.

Queen's Palace - Mentioned in Grants Pass *Courier* in 1886. Located "on second floor," probably near 110 Exit but the 1907 photograph (Watson, 1909) labeled with this name is of Paradise Lost. Name used by *Observer* (1906), Name used 1897-1917. Names by Joaquin Miller during Kincaid/Miller/Watson expedition of 1907 (Miller, 1909).

Queen's Reception Room - North of Petrified Forest. Name by Rowley (1916) still in use.

Queen's Throne - In Paradise Alley, name by Rowley, 1916.

Rachel's Well - Name by Miller (1909) during Kincaid/Miller/Watson expedition of 1907 on "first floor" of cave.

Rainy Cavern - Unknown cave location. Mentioned by Michelson in 1891 EXAMINER article. *See* chapter 2.

Rain-in-the-face - Old name for formation in high area of Royal Gorge (Macduff, 1917).

Ram's Head - Recent name in Imagination Room.

Rat Hole - Named since 1930. It has a 50 degree, slick slope. Once mostly filled with fill. It lies along a fault upward from the Sand Room.

Rebecca's Well - Unknown cave location, named by Smith, 1911. The cave guide told one group of visitors that eyeless fish were caught here with grapple hooks. They resembled eels more than fish. Since the government took over the caves, no fishing has been allowed inside the caves.

Reception Room - Old name (Rowley, 1913-1917) for Faerie Ballroom.

Rip Van Winkle's Chamber - Unknown cave location, name by Rowley, 1913-1917.

River of Fire - 1934 Rowley name for River Styx in Ghost Room.

River Styx - Called "the Stygian" in 1907. First used by Joaquin Miller and Chandler B. Watson (1909). Once emerged from the cave near the cave's entrance, the stream takes the name Cave Creek. *See* Cave Creek.

Rock Hanging From Ceiling - Old name for Widow Maker (Rowley, 1933, *Oregon Journal*, 1938).

Roosevelt's Canyon - For Theodore Roosevelt, President of the United States. Rowley name 1913-1917 for area below and south of Bridge over the River Styx.

Roosevelt's Ride - Same as Roosevelt's Rough Ride. First named by Joaquim Miller during Kincaid/Miller/Watson expedition of 1907 (Miller, 1909) and still in use.

Roosevelt's Rough Ride - Old name for Devil's Backbone, a steep "ridge" formerly in old tour connection between Watson's Grotto and the Imagination Room. Largely destroyed during cave renovation by CCC's in mid-1930's. Also known as Roosevelt's Rough Ride (Meyers, 1907), Teddy's Rough Ride (Rowley, 1913-17) and Satan's Backbone.

Rotten Rock Dome - North side of East Ghost Room Annex.

Royal Gorge - Before Imagination Room on main tour route. Name by Rowley (1916) still in use. The northern end is near the surface. Visited by Rowley's tours. 387 feet surveyed in 1971.

Samson's Coffin - Breakdown area between Dry Room and Imagination Room on tour (Nickerson, 1914).

Sand Room - Bottom of Rat Hole. West of Shovel Room in southern part of cave. 1966 name still in use (Knutson, 1975).

Santa Claus - Recent name in Imagination Room.

Satan's Backbone - Old name for Devil's Backbone.

Satan's Slide - 1907-1924 name for Devil's Slide.

Satan's Soup Bowl - "lower caves" (Tebben, 1917).

Scalp Rock - Ceiling rock once located just before entering Grand Column area, since removed. Same as Old Scalp Rock.

Scatterbrains - Recent name for low ceiling rock above Clobberstone.

Seneca Lake - East of original Niagara Falls. There can be soft mud in the "lake" or water (August, 1985). Between Seneca Lake and the Paradise Alley Extension is a foot long soda straw column. Helictites and collars on columns are also present. Gours occur west of the Lake. A mouse? jaw occurs in a narrow alcove south of Seneca Lake.

The Sharkhead - Unknown cave location, 1907. Between the 110 Exit and the Wind Tunnel (Josephine County Caves, 1915).

Shark's Jaw - Near 110 Exit, Named by Miller during Kincaid/Miller/Watson expedition of 1907 (Miller, 1909); name by used by Rowley, 1913-1917.

Shepherd's Dell - Across from Snow White, had algae growing on it. (Dunham, 1939).

Shortcut Passage - Connects Wigwam Room with Petrified Garden.

Shovel Room - Between South Room and South Ghost Room Annex, just before South Complex.

Shower Bath - Rowley's (1917) and District Forester's name (1917) for Rainy Cavern.

Shower Room - East of East Ghost Room Annex. Tours no longer regularly visit here. Named in 1966. A fault may control the orientation of this room (Knutson, 1970).

Sidehill Gouger - In Wedding Cake Room (Dunham, 1939).

Sign of Zorro - In Kudgel's Cave.

Signature Room - Near or in the South Room. Name on 1966 map.

Siphon - 1966 map shows it at the end of the River Styx down Jules Verne Well. Going down Jules Verne Well described in Chapter 2.

Slab Crawl - North of Sand Room (Knutson, 1975).

Slime Monster - Recent name for Jaws of Death.

Small Dome - Adjacent to Balcony Room in south end of cave.

Snow White - Near Niagara Falls "on the chasm brink to the left." (Dunham, 1939). Snow White and the Seven Dwarfs includes several smaller stalagmites.

Snowflake Room - Recrystallized stalactites by Niagara Falls.

Solomon's Bedstead - Unknown cave location. Mentioned in Examiner expedition of 1894. See chapter 2 (page 66).

Solomon's Temple - 1907 and 1913-17 name for Ghost Room. During Kincaid/Miller/Watson expedition of 1907, this room was measured to be 350x150x80 feet. (Miller, 1909).

Source of Cave Creek - District Forester's (1917) name for Cave Creek starting at Main Entrance. *See* Cave Creek.

South Canyon Passage - South of the last natural room before Exit Tunnel.

South End - Above Rathole level. 201 feet surveyed in 1971.

South Ghost Room Annex - 486 feet surveyed in 1971.

South Room - Large room at extreme southern end of known cave. Name on 1966 map.

Sparkplug - Name for Barney Google's horse. Perhaps in Imagination Room

(Saunders, 1924). Barney Google was a popular comic strip during the 1920's-1930's.

Specimen Chamber - Between 110 Exit and Hell's Gate, named in 1888.

Spitting Rock Dome - In North Ghost Room Annex.

Spitting Stone - Recent name for indented stalagmite on Ghost Room Terrace. Refer to Bow of Battleship *Oregon*.

Spook Parlor - Unknown cave location, name by Rowley, 1913-1917.

Squeeze - Called Fat Lady's Squeeze" in 1934. Finch (1934) recommends that "some work should be done to improved dangerous places and the picturesque squeezes and low bridges should be left."

The Star Chamber - On "second floor," named by Miller during Kincaid/Miller /Watson expedition of 1907 (Miller, 1909). May be near 110 Exit.

Steamboat Chamber - 1888 name for some room between Imagination Room and Beehive Room, possibly Adam's Tomb or part of the Royal Gorge.

Stone's Falls - West of East Ghost Room Annex. Named in 1894, although name could refer to two different places in cave. Named after cave explorer Colonel Stone. For description *see* Chapter 2.

Spitting Rock Dome - In North Ghost Room Annex.

Stream Grotto - Stream area in Ghost Room. It was the name for Dante's Inferno on 1966 and 1974 maps.

Stream Passage - It begins beneath and a little to the west of the Shower Room and about 40 feet below it and proceeds north for about 100 feet at a gentle gradient where it comes to an abrupt end with the stream disappearing into a crack in the floor.

(The) Stygian - 1907 (Miller/Watson, 1909) name for the River Styx. *See* Chapter 1.

Sucker Creek - Named by miners from Illinois, whose state's nickname was the Sucker State. An older name for the creek is Little Grayback Creek.

Sullivan's Hallway - Unknown cave location mentioned by Michelson in 1894 EXAMINER article. Name honors boxer John L. Sullivan. Chapter 2.

Sunset Point - Area just outside the Exit Tunnel. Rowley by 1939 used the name to refer to the area off to the left of the first sharp turn upon leaving the Monument.

Suspended Ceiling - Old name for Kincaid's Dance Hall (Dunham, 1939), probably named by Rowley.

Table Rock - Near Mount Pitt (*Oregon Journal*, July 1, 1923) on right of winter route opposite beginning of Rimstone Room. "Table Rocks" (2) prominent geological formations are due north of the Medford Airport.

Tall Man's Misery - Railings installed here in 1961. In 1963, the trail here was lowered 14 inches and the name is deleted from the tour.

Teddy's Rough Ride - Old name for Devil's Backbone.

Telephone Booth - May be near Lake Michigan. (*Oregon Journal*, July 1, 1923).

Theatrical Stage - 1907 to 1915 name for all or part of Ghost Room. Joaquin Miller lists this in his inventory of places visited during Kincaid/Miller/ Watson expedition of 1907, (1909).Called the present name by 1913.

Three Amigos - Same as Three Stooges.

The Three Sisters - Possibly in Wedding Cake Room, name by Rowley, 1916-1917.

Three Stooges - Ghost Room above Terrace. Also called (in part) the White Faerie Castle.

Tomb of Rameses the Third - Near Ghost Room, named by John O. Quinn of the *Examiner* 1894 expedition; an "ante-chamber" of the Ghost Room, possibly Joaquin Miller's Chapel. *See* Chapter 2.

Toy Room - Near Joaquin Miller's Chapel, 1913, Nickerson, 1914. Possibly the Paradise Alley Extension.

Transformer Passage - Near 110 Exit, 79 feet long surveyed in 1971.

Treasure of Monte Cristo Room - In annex of Junction Room. See Monte Cristo's Treasure Chamber.

Treasurer's Chamber - On "second floor." Named by Miller during Kincaid/ Miller/ Watson expedition of 1907 (Miller, 1909). Name used by Rowley, 1913-1917.

Treasury Vaults - 1914 name for Paradise Lost.

Tree Root - Inside cave on left not far from Main entrance.

Tripstone - Ghost Room Terrace.

Troll - Recent name in Imagination Room.

Twin Sisters - Double-topped stalagmite near Lake Michigan in the Shasta Room. 1897 name still in use. Named Twin Sisters by Rowley (1916) and Kate and Duplicate (1934).

Two Little Owls - Called Max and Climax. Near Jacob's Well and Mother Owl (Dunham, 1939).

Unnamed Chamber - Old name (Josephine County Caves, 1915) for Paradise Lost.

Upper Entrance - From 1885 to 1920's, name for 110 Exit.

Upper Level - Above Devil's Slide. It appears to have developed along a slightly inclined bedding plane.

Upper Bone Room - Extreme SW end of known cave.

Ursine Catacombs - 1894 name for Bone Dome.

Valley of the Moon - Right behind the Wishing Post.

Vegetable Room - 1913-1917 Rowley name for Petrified Gardens.

Vineyard - Near 110 Exit, *ca.* 1924.

Washington Monument - Stalagmite in Joaquin Miller's Chapel, 4 feet high, first named in 1897.

Washington Statue - Named by Miller (1909), same as Washington Monument. A "circular tower 6 feet in diameter and 50 feet high, in the Toy Room, was called George Washington. (Nickerson, 1914). Name possibly for Bird of Paradise, on the way down from the Golden Stairs (Macduff, 1917). A 1934 map placed it in the Head Hunter's Trophy Room.

Water Whelp - Tributary of Panther Spring that begins above the Big Tree. Probably results from contact between quartz diorite and argillite. Origin of name unknown.

Waterfall Passage - North of first clay pocket in Exit Tunnel. Name on 1966 map. 231 feet surveyed in 1971.

Watson's Gorge - Named for spelunking colleague Chandler B. Watson by John Kincaid in 1907 while a part of the Kincaid/Miller/Watson expedition of 1907 (Miller, 1909). Old name for Watson's Grotto.

Watson's Grotto - 92 feet from Entrance, 4 feet higher, 65 feet below surface, named by Rowley in 1916, formerly called Watson's Gorge.

Wedding Cake - Formation in Wedding Cake Room. Name appeared on a map. Originally called Horsetail Falls.

Wedding Cake Room - 1,910 feet' from Entrance, 130 feet higher, 170 feet below surface. Name in use by 1966.

(Weird) Ghost Chamber - See Ghost Chamber. The "weird" suffix was used in a 1913 newspaper article.

Whale's Passage - 1934 name for Passageway of the Whale.

White Faerie Castle - Ghost Room above Terrace.

White Formation Passage - Part of old commercial tour, connects South Ghost Room Annex with last natural room before Exit Tunnel. Visited by Rowley's tours.

White House - Across route from Banana Grove. Named by Rowley in 1916. Name still on 1938 map. Now named Pipe Organ, perhaps because frequent touching has dulled the color.

White Room - Unknown cave location, 1902, 1913.

Whitfield Dome - In Shovel Room in southern end of cave (Knutson, 1975).

Widow Maker - Large wedged-in breakdown block on ceiling near Ghost Room Terrace, Rowley's name from 1934 to present.

Wiggle (or Wriggle) Holes - Near Wind Tunnel and after Paradise Alley, 1916 to 1920's.

Wigwam - 1934 map name for Imagination Room.

Windy Passage - Named by Joaquin Miller during Kincaid/Miller/Watson expedition of 1907 (Miller, 1909). still in use in 1915, now called Wind Tunnel.

Winter Scene in the Yukon - In White Formation Passage, probably also called Yukon River.

Wishing Post - The (Old) Wishing Post, first so named in 1934, was called ("Old) Satan's Hitching Post" from 1916 to the mid-1920's. Dick Rowley, a guide, made the wish to always come out of the cave alive.

Witherspoon's Hole. For details refer to Balcony Room.

Yosemite (Park) - Near Bridal Veil Falls and Exit Tunnel (Dunham, 1939). Also called Yosemite Falls (Rowley, 1916).

Yukon River - In White Formation Passage, name by Rowley, 1934. Probably also called Winter Scene in the Yukon (Dunham, 1939).

Zephyr Path - 1906 name for Wind Tunnel and Crater Lake Passage? - called "Windy Passage in 1907 and 1915-1916 and Cave of the Winds on 1966 and 1974 maps.

◇

Appendix F
Visitor Count
Oregon Caves National Monument
National Park Service

Over 4,780,000 people have visited the Monument during the periods covered in this report.

Calculations are based on monthly readings of traffic counter and averages of people per car random counts for summer, fall, winter and spring seasons.

Based on the numbers in the chart, the survey showed that 57 percent of visitors had not been to the caves in three years. 38 percent were first time visitors. Less than 1% had been to the caves before the last three years.

Ages of those interviewed were well-distributed across all age groups with half in age categories of 40-49 years or younger. Visitors who live within 50 miles of the interview site tend to be younger than visitors who live more than 50 miles away.

Visitation by years for which data is available

Year	Visitors to Monument	Visitors on Cave Tours	Remarks
	→Erratic data earlier than 1923←		
1909	no data	360	
1910	no data	367	
1911	no data	256	
1916	no data	1,000 est.	
1920	1.800 est.	no data	
1921	1,900 est.	no data	
1922	10,000 est.	no data	
1923	19,630	14,724	
1924	21,842	16,381	
1925	18,765	14,074	
1926	25,466	19,630	
1927	24,466	18,597	
1928	21,710	28,947	
1929	36,365	27,266	
1930	35,469	26,491	
1931	37,932	28,469	Caves lighted
1932	23,2345	17,434	Drop due to Depression
1933	19,573	14,680	Low point in Depression years
1934	30,480	22,860	Chateau (lodge) opens. Monument transferred to National Parks
1935	32,484	24,363	
1936	55,424	41,568	
1937	59,434	44,567	
1938	53,784	40,348	
1939	62,018	46,513	
1940	59,927	44,945	
1941	61,680	46,260	
1942	20,590	15,443	Wartime travel restrictions
1943	3,914	2,939	Low point in World War-II years
1944	4,569	3,427	Wartime travel restrictions
1945	23,403	17,552	Wartime restrict lifted in mid-summer
1946	86,349	64,761	
1947	98,129	73,597	
1948	86,349	64,761	
1949	98,790	74,093	
1950	91,520	68,640	
1951	95,779	68,128	
1952	76,599	69,861	
1953	69,861	60,014	
1954	80,888	60,666	
1955	83,007	62,255	
1956	79,886	59.914	

Year	Visitors to Monument	Visitors* on Cave Tours	Remarks
1957	85,265	63,949	
1958	80,019	60,014	
1959	86,428	65,267	39 bus tours
1960	101,345	68,256	
1961	102,940	74,266	
1962	129,074	92,112	
1963	125,799	79,016	
1964	149,926	90,466	Flood. Major damage to buildings
1965	130,891	80,770	Nat'l Mon. closed 90 days due to flood
1966	150,284	96,655	
1967	128,355	no data	Millionth visitor recorded
1968	no data	100,000 est.	
1969	no data	no data	
1970	160,000	107,210	First time cave visits exceed 100,000
1971	179,572	114,590	
1972	199,434	123,331	Highest visitation up to 1995
1973	177,000	116,000 est.	
1974	152,286	96,935	Energy crisis reduces visitation
1975	159,203	100,745	
1976	172,517	116,242	
1977	181,870	114,958	Tours: $2.50/adult, $1.25/children
1978	173,130	110,489	
1979	131,318	78.277	
1980	129,760	no data	Tours: $3.75/adult, $2.25/children
1981	136,085	no data	
1982	115,953	no data	
1983	114,805	no data	Three millionth visitor recorded
1984	119,258	no data	
1985	94,668	no data	
1986	102,568	no data	
1987	103,600	no data	
1988	117,525	no data	
1989	103,597	no data	
1990	99,638	no data	
1991	99,541	no data	
1992	86,607	no data	
1993	97,743	no data	
1994	97,806	5,089	
1995	103,576	65,282	
1996	98,903	64,991	Tours:** $6.00/adult, $3.50/children
1997	84,704	57,692	74 bus tours

* Cave visits for which there were paid admissions. Totals do not include school, or special groups guided by National Park Service or complimentary tours.
**Prices of admission tickets to the cave may change without notice.

Appendix G
Geology: The Creation of a Cave and Formation of Marble

Decoratives in the Oregon Caves

What is a rock?

A rock is any relatively hard naturally formed mineral mass or aggregate. Rocks are classified first by how they were formed and, within those classifications, by minerals they contain.

There are six basic rock types each determined by how the rock was formed. The rock classifications are:

1.) Plutonic igneous	4.) chemical sedimentary
2.) volcanic igneous	5.) regional metamorphic
3.) clastic sedimentary	6.) contact metamorphic

Examples of each of these six rock types may be found in the Oregon Caves. Igneous rocks are formed from molten rock that has been forced up through the earth's crust.

Plutonic ingenious rock forms when the molten rock does not reach the earth's surface but cools underground. Being insulated by the surrounding rock, this molten material cools slowly allowing time for large crystals to grow.

Volcanic igneous rocks form when the molten rock actually reaches the earth's surface. Contact with air and reduced pressure promotes rapid cooling allowing only limited crystal growth. Some molten material cools so quickly that no crystals form. The resulting rock is known as volcanic glass – obsidian.

In Oregon Caves an example of Plutonic igneous rock is found in the Ghost Room with the quartz diorite dike. Illustrations of volcanic igneous rock in Oregon Caves are the thin layers of volcanic ash exposed in the wall just behind the Spitting Stone at the Ghost Room overlook.

Sedimentary rocks form from weathering of pre-existing rocks and the subsequent movement and redisposition of the eroded material. The weathered material can be transported by wind, gravity or, as is most often the case by water. Once redeposited, the process by which the

181

Calcite crystals in layer of flowstone (8 inches high).

particles are changed to rock is called *lithification.* This is a chemical process that reduces the original porosity (ratio of the volume of void space to the total volume of a sediment or rock).

In limestone, the most important lithification process is cementation rather than compaction. In other words, the reduction of pore space in limestone from the filling in of existing pores with lime cement is greater than the reduction of pore space from the pressures associated with the weight of overlaying material.

There are two classifications of sedimentary rocks:

         1.) clastic   2.) chemical.

Clastic sedimentary rock results when loose sediments are laid down by water, gravity, wind or other mechanical methods.

Chemical sedimentary rocks form when sediments precipitate out of a solution to form a solid mass.

Examples: Clastic sedimentary rock at Oregon Caves would be the cemented gravel near the Grand Column. All the cave formations are of chemical sedimentary rocks.

Metamorphic rocks are rocks that have been altered by heat, stress, pressure, or a combination of these conditions which cause the rock to recrystallize without actually melting. Sedimentary, igneous, or metamorphic rocks can undergo the changes to become new metamorphic rocks.

Metamorphic rocks also come in two types:

1.) regional   2.) contact

Regional metamorphic rocks undergo transformation over a large area similar to baking a potato in an oven where the whole potato is affected more or less evenly. An illustration of a regional metamorphic rock in Oregon Caves would be the cave marble which is metamorphosed limestone.

Contact metamorphic rocks are changed by direct contact with a heat source such as igneous dike and can be readily compared to the cooking of a hamburger. When frying a hamburger, the side closest to the heat source cooks more completely than the distant side from the heat.

An example of contact metamorphic rock would be the marble closest to the argillite in the Connecting Tunnel which was cooked a second time with the intrusion of the hot argillitic clays.

Formation of the Oregon Caves Marble

The origin of the marble in Oregon Caves began between 150 and 220 million years ago, near the beginning of the dinosaur era. The cave marble formed within an enclosed ocean basin ringed on one side by the continent and on the other side by an island arc. Numerous creatures lived and died in the basin. Many of these critters secreted calcium carbonate shells that settled to the bottom as the critters died.

Foraminifera, single-celled animals, were undoubtedly the most numerous. Their shells and the less abundant shells of the larger sea life created a layer of limy ooze in the ocean basin. This ooze was recrystallized into a somewhat fossiliferous limestone.

The Oregon Caves National Monument is located near the boundary of two sections of the earth's crust known as plates. The ocean basin in which the cave marble was deposited, was destroyed as the

North American plate collided with the Pacific Ocean plate. The force of the collision of the plates bent and folded the basin sediments to begin mountain formation.

The Pacific Ocean plate, being heavier than the continental plate, sank under the continental plate. As the ocean plate was pushed down (also known as subduction), it was heated and partially melted. Some of this melted rock made its way back toward the surface as volcanoes, plutons, or dikes. The upwelling magma further lifted the basin sediments into mountains and transformed them with heat.

The heat from the ascending magma metamorphosed the basin limestone re-crystallizing it into marble. Although limestone and marble have the same mineral composition, mostly calcium carbonate or calcite, the crystal structure is altered by the cooking of the limestone.

Other single-cell animals known as *radiolarinn* manufactured shells of silica. As they died, their skeletons helped build layers of silica muck which was later recrystallized into chert. The chert layers are readily visible in the cave. Made of silica, rather than readily soluble limestone or marble, these layers resist erosion and develop prominent ledges in the cave walls.

Although the cave marble was initially created by the shells and skeletons of sea creatures, few fossils are found in the marble. There are two main reasons for this.

1.) Numerous skeletal remains are destroyed by the process of *lithification*. The same process that solidified the limy ooze recrystallized the fossil remains destroying their structures.

2.) The metamorphism further recrystallized the rock destroying more of the preserved remnants.

Creation of a Cave

The water table is the top zone beneath the earth's surface where the ground is fully saturated with water. All rock, though it seems solid, contains pores (open space). Water can travel within and between these pore places. Some rock has a much higher ratio of open space to total rock and is said to be porous. If the rock allows water to readily travel between its pores, it is permeable.

When it rains or snow melts, the water may evaporate, run off, and collect in surface drainages, or make its way to the water table. Water headed for the water table filters its way down through soils and permeable rock until it collects above an impermeable rock layer thus forming the zone of saturation and the water table.

The level of the water table responds to several variables. The water table reacts to the volume of precipitation within an area and is not constantly at a certain level. During periods of prolonged drought, the water table will drop and with sustained rainfall will rise. The water table is affected by topography and the surface features of an area. On hilltops, the water table is usually further below the surface than it is in adjacent valleys. In the mountains of southwestern Oregon, there is an average rainfall of 50 inches each year therefore there was plenty of water available as well as the right kind of rock to form the Oregon Caves.

Where the water table meets the surface, there you might find a river, stream, pond, swamp or a spring.

Water Zones

Vadose zone is that part of the earth between the surface and the water table. Here water moves *vertically* under the force of gravity.

Phreatic zone is the earth below the water table. Water flows nearly *horizontally* here. A well is dug from the surface into the *phreatic* zone to tap its water. Phreatic water is charged with mild acids that are not harmful to people. The dripping water in the caves is phreatic water which is mild carbonic acid. It is also found in bottled soda pop.

Water from the surface will find its way to the water table by the path of least resistance, that is, along cracks, fractures, layers of more permeable rock, bedding planes, etc. Near the surface, the water will combine with carbon dioxide from decaying organic material to form a weak acid – carbonic acid ($H_2O + CO_2 = H_2CO_3$). As the water (H_2O) continues to move downward, soluble material may be dissolved to form caves. As the dissolved cavity becomes larger, a disproportionate amount of water will be diverted to the new easy path of least resistance and the cavity will grow.

Once water has initiated dissolution, cavities may grow larger through a process called breakdown – rock that falls due to natural processes. Breakdown can occur through a variety of mechanisms. The two most significant are acidic water corroding away at rocks supporting material and drainage of water from a water filled passage. In the second instance, the rock requires the buoyancy from the water to maintain its attachment to the wall or ceiling. The water gone, the rock falls.

The largest caves in the world occur in limestone. This is largely calcite and is readily dissolved by weak acid like carbonic acid. Some good examples of limestone caves are Carlsbad Caverns in southeastern New Mexico, Lehman Caves in Great Basin National Park in Nevada, Mammoth caves in Kentucky. Caves can occur in nearly any rock type. The Oregon Caves occur in marble. The caves in Lava Beds National Monument in Northern California, Craters of the Moon National Monument in Idaho, Gardner Cave State Park in northeastern Washington, and Sunset Crater National Monument in northern Arizona are lava tube caves. Glacial ice caves are within Mount Rainier National Park near Tacoma, Washington and at Denali National Park in Alaska. The Pinnacles National Monument in California is volcanic tuff.

Decorating the Cave

Caves are said to have two possible futures; both result in the destruction of the caves. Given enough time, and erosional power, the ceiling of the cave may be removed or caved into the cave chambers. With enough time, an intact ceiling, an open exchange of air from the outside, a flow of acidic water, and a source of calcium carbonate, the cave may become filled with cave "decorations."

When the right conditions exist, formations in a cave can start to form. The requirements include:

1.) A hole or cavity or a cave within the rock

2.) Water coming into the open space that is acidic and contains dissolved calcium carbonate. (NOTE: Although moist formations are deposited from water-conveyed lime, some formations may be deposited by air-carried moisture that contains small amounts of dissolved calcite.)

3.) An opening to the hole, cavity or cave that allows dissemination of carbon dioxide

4.) Time

The process begins as precipitation falls on the earth's surface as rain or snow. As in cave dissolution, it picks up carbon dioxide from decaying organic material. The acidic water percolating through rock layers containing calcium carbonate dissolves the lime then carries it downward into the cave. As the water enters the cave, it may behave in a number of ways. The behavior of the water decides which cave deposits develop. As persons observe in the Oregon Caves, as pointed out by the guides, both stalactites and stalagmites grow because of dripping water. The rate of the water flow and amount of evaporation are two factors that assist in determining whether a stalactite (hangs

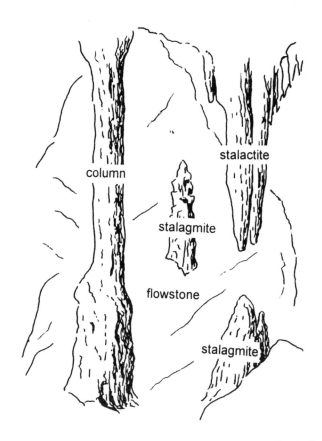

column

stalactite

stalagmite

flowstone

stalagmite

from a ceiling) or stalagmite (builds up from the floor) forms. As a general rule, water dripping rapidly will not stay on the ceiling long enough to deposit a stalactite.

As the water laden with dissolved calcium carbonate enters the open space of the cave, pressure is released and carbon dioxide returns to its gaseous state, escaping from the water droplet. As the volume of carbon dioxide in the water droplet decreases so does the acidity. This can be compared to the opening of a soda pop bottle and the rush of carbon dioxide bubbles that escape the soft drink. The lower the acidity, the less calcium carbonate can stay in solution leaving the calcium carbonate to precipitate out of the water as cave formations. Air flow moving past the water droplet expedites the removal of carbon dioxide and the lowering of the acidity, therefore increasing formation growth.

Stalactites and stalagmites

Stalactites usually begin as soda straws, which are hollow tubes of calcite formed as calcite deposits around the outside of the water drop-let. The diameter of the opening inside the soda straw is usually equivalent to the size of the drop of water. As the soda straw grows, something (a calcite crystal, a piece of clay, etc.) may plug the opening. Water is then forced to flow down the outside of the soda straw making it wider and the formation takes on an icicle or carrot shape. It is wider at the top and pointed at the bottom.

Stalagmites may or may not have a corresponding stalactite. Even though the water may have deposited some calcite on the ceiling, it can still deposit more on the floor. As the water is churned, it will lose additional carbon dioxide and deposit more calcite. Think of popping the top of a soda pop after it has been shaken. The release of carbon dioxide can be almost explosive.

Draperies

Draperies are formed on sloped ceilings and walls where the water coming in rather than dropping immediately from its entry will flow along the incline for some distance leaving behind a streak of calcite. As the water travels, dips or protuberances in its course may cause the deposit to curve. The precipitate will eventually form a vertical sheet of calcite. Drapery formations can be compared to water running down one's arm from wet hands as one reaches for a towel. The water follows the slope until gravity pulls it away and the water drop falls away.

Flowstone

Flowstone is deposited where water flows as a sheet along a surface. The surface may be a ceiling, floor or wall. As the water travels, it releases carbon dioxide and deposits calcite across the slope. Flowstone tends to have a smooth or undulating veneer. Marks on walls left over one hundred years ago by visitors in the Oregon Caves, may eventually be completely covered by the continued growth of flowstone.

Rimstone

Rimstone dams form under conditions similar to flowstone. The distinction is as the water is flowing it is unevenly agitated as it hits irregularities or bumps on the floor. More calcite will build upwards along the jagged edges than elsewhere and will act as "dams." Water backs up behind the "dams" until it spills over depositing additional limestone on the leading edge of the building ridge. Rimstone dams tend to lean (tilt) into the direction from which the water is flowing.

Helictites

Cave formations which twist and bend or have offshoots like limbs are called helictites. These have a central canal through which water flows just as occurs with a soda straw stalactite. The exact reason for the variance in the formation remains a mystery but several theories exist. One suggests that water flows through a helictite under capillary pressure. The pressure alters crystal deposits causing unusual crystal growth. High rates of evaporation also appear to be prerequisite to helictite development.

Cave Rafts

Thin plates of calcium carbonate, called Cave Rafts, form on cave pools. The plates float on the water by surface tension until they grow too large and sink or float to the pool edge where they may become attached. The upper sides of the calcite rafts are smooth and glossy while the bottom side is covered with rough crystals. If cave raft development is extensive, the rafts may grow together over a pool's surface. This development of a thin surface overlaying an active or dried up pool is called "cave ice."

Shelfstone

Shelfstone occurs similarly to cave rafts. Small ledges of calcite build up near the edges of a pool. More carbon dioxide is lost as small waves from water dripping into the pool make contact with the cave walls and the water is agitated, precipitating limestone. A previous water level is evidenced by the presence of shelfstone.

Cave popcorn (coralloids)

As with so many cave formations, there are numerous theories as to how cave popcorn may form. In fact, different examples of cave popcorn may indeed form in very different ways. This adornment may form when water falling from the ceiling splashes. As it splashes, it can sprinkle water droplets across a wide area. If these droplets contain dissolved calcium carbonate, then small amounts of calcite may be deposited with each drop. The result is a splatter array of bumpy nodules of calcite – popcorn.

Cave popcorn may form from the condensation of cool moisture laden air onto walls, ceilings, floors and pre-existing formations. As the water condenses onto a surface, small amounts of calcite may be deposited and the cave popcorn formed.

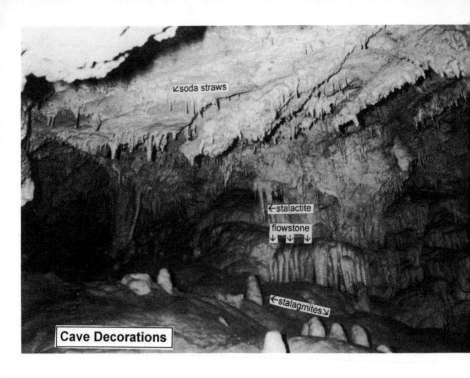

Cave Decorations

(labels in image: soda straws, stalactite, flowstone, stalagmites)

Popcorn can also form under water or from the slow seepage of water from cave walls. In the Oregon Caves, popcorn is formed mostly from evaporation and slow seepage of water on the walls. Most of this popcorn points toward cave entrances where cold air enters in winter and warms. As the air warms, the relative humidity drops and water is evaporated from the near side of the cave formations depositing popcorn.

Mondmilch

A cave mud consisting mostly of calcite and water is called mondmilch. When dry, the composition must be more than ninety percent calcite. Looking soft and pasty when wet, mondmilch resembles cottage cheese when dry. The calcite crystals in mondmilch are very small and are suspended in water.

Fibers of fungal material are sometimes found associated with mondmilch. The relationship between the two is uncertain. It is possible that mondmilch growth is enhanced through the life cycle of the fungus and its breakdown of minerals in the rock walls. Likewise, it is possible that the presence of the mondmilch increases fungal development by providing food. High rates of evaporation and intermediate rates of seepage are also related to mondmilch development. The largest concentrations of mondmilch are found in areas of the cave that are relatively dry and have high air flow. High rate of evaporation may be causing rapid deposition of calcite and the growth of small crystals.

Boxwork

A network of lines of crystals that protrude from a ceiling due to their greater resistance to solution forms a boxwork. Often found near faults where the marble is cracked, boxwork forms when these cracks fill with large calcite crystals. The marble, consisting of small calcite crystals, is readily corroded, more and more of the lines of crystals are exposed as they standout from the adjacent ceiling.

Rate of Growth

Each formation in a cave has a different rate of growth which is determined by numerous factors. These include rate of water seepage, acidity of the water, airflow past the formation, amounts of dissolved calcite, etc. Although average growth rates may be determined, any formation will probably not be growing at this rate. Most formations will grow either faster or slower than an average. These growth rates are often not consistent. As environmental conditions change, so will the speed at which formations develop. Therefore, average rates of growth will fluctuate over time.

Colors of Formations

Pure calcite is clear. Any color on a calcite crystal or formation is the result of some other ingredient or refractant being added. When calcite appears white (milky) it is the result of trapped air or water bubbles within the structure. Reds, browns, tans, are a result of organic material, or rust, being added to the composition. Acidic water may carry with it organic or mineral substances and iron oxide depositing it with the calcite.

Clay Worms (vermiculations)

Wormlike deposits of loose irregular shaped material found on walls ceilings and floors of caves are vermiculations (clay worms). The unconsolidated materials are most often mud and clay but they can also be lint, carbon or algae. Clay worms develop as thin films of water evaporate from the cave surface. A static electric charge on the clay or lint particles draws them together with other similar fragments and a thin discontinuous deposit forms. In the Oregon Caves many of the clay worm deposits are inactive (that is, no longer wet) and some are covered by a thin later of calcite. ◇

Appendix H
TIMELINE — OREGON CAVES

1828   During the summer, the first recorded presence of non-native people in the Siskiyou Mountains is by a Hudsons Bay Company expedition in search of furs.

1850   Oregon Governor Joseph Lane, former Superintendent of Indian Affairs for Oregon and Washington, negotiates peace treaty with 150 Takelma Indians in the Rogue River Valley (not ratified).

1851   Discoveries of gold near Kerby and at Jacksonville* (six miles west of Medford**) brings hoards of non-native miners to the Siskiyou Mountains to the distress of Indians.

1874   While on a hunting trip in the fall of the year, Elijah Davidson is believed to have been the first person to enter what is now named the Oregon Caves. His dog was chasing a bear, and the two animals disappeared into a hole in the side of the mountain. The route to the cave was up Williams Creek from the east then over a shoulder on Grayback Mountain. It is not established how far Davidson went inside the cave. On this outing he was accompanied by his brother Carter, Julius Godwin who married Elijah's sister; Jimmie Dale; a person named Moses; and possibly two others. According to Davidson's account, he baited the cave entrance with a freshly killed deer to attract the bear, then he killed the bear after it emerged the following day.

In 1913, Davidson recalled that he returned to the cave the next day with Ira Sparlin, John Kincaid and David Jones to explore the cave. When they arrived, they found the bear he had shot the day before. Some confusion as to the date arises as some evidence suggests this trip was in 1877. Rita Elliot claims Ira Sparlin may have arrived at the cave the same day as the initial discovery or a day or so later. Further confusion is evident with the recollection of Winter Davidson, who believed that Elijah, Carter, and David John Sr., came back to the cave a year later.

---

* For the history of Jacksonville refer to bibliography for *Jacksonville, Oregon; Antique Town in a Modern Age.*

** For the history of Medford refer to bibliography for *The Lure of Medford.*

192

Michelson, writing in the San Francisco *Examiner* 1891, after an expedition to the caves, claims Elijah Davidson returned the day after the discovery and lighted his way with a pine torch during which trip he became lost for four hours breaking stalactites to mark the way he had come. He finally left the cave out a different hole than the one he entered.

1877   Cave trips. Depending on the writer, the visitors to the caves vary and the dates of the visits often seem unsure. With Mr. William W. Fidler, Elijah Davidson explored the cave. Fidler wrote in 1877 in the *Morning Oregonian* (Portland, Ore.) that "the stalactites and stalagmites surpass anything ever dreamed of and nothing I ever beheld in Nature before so completely overcame me with suggestions of sublimity and beauty.... It looked like a shame to desecrate or deface anything so beautiful...." (*See* Chapter 1.)

Fidler wrote from recollection, 45 years later, that Elijah Davidson, Carter Davidson, James Nail were there together. He claims that during a hunting trip, these men used pitch pine torches for light. They made ladders from small trees then tied a rope to the entrance so they would not get lost. One writer (Sweet) claims this was the first trip into the cave by Elijah Davidson after his discovery of the cave in 1874. However Fidler wrote from memory in the *Oregon Historical Quarterly* (Sept. 1922), that along with Elijah Davidson, Carter Davidson and James Nail were Mrs. Julius Goodwin, Frank Rose and two [teenagers] David Johns Jr. and Ira Sparlin.

Some further cloudiness occurs with the writing of Watson in 1909 who claims on the first trip, after the discovery of the cave, the visitors were Davidson, John H. Kincaid, Frank M. Nickerson and John M. Chapman. Fidler, writing in 1877 says the visit was on July 5th. Fidler, writing in 1909, indicated he went with Simpson on an all day horseback ride to the cave from a cabin near the head of Williams Creek. Frank Nickerson claims to have also visited the cave with Davidson and John M. Chapman during the year.

What is known as the "110 Exit" is discovered.

1878   At least three parties arrive in August at the same time. These included the Robert A. Miller group. These visitors used balls of string to find their way out.

1879   Carter T. Davidson, Elijah's brother, signed his name inside the cave apparently with smoke from a torch.

1880   Homer and Ernest Harkness, brothers, took a squatter's claim at the lower entrance to the cave, according to Watson (1909).

1883   In September, Dr. Thomas Condon, Ph. D., for many years the Professor of Geology and Natural History at the University of Oregon, and known as The Grand Geologist of Oregon, was the honored guest member of a small party that explored the caves. Others in the party were W. W. Cardwell, Ben B. Beekman, Frank R. Neil and George W. Dunn, all from Jackson County and students in a geology class taught by Dr. Condon, and Jim Birdsey (at that time sheriff of Jackson County). See Appendix for full text of a short narrative written at the time by George Dunn.

1885   Homer Harkness and his brother-in-law Walter C. Burch (1859-1935) of Leland, Oregon, took out a mineral claim on 160 acres surrounding the cave. They were unable to acquire title because the land was unsurveyed. They spent about $1,000 enlarging passages and building surface trails during the next two years. The cost to visit the cave, which included camping, "medicinal" cave waters, and good pasture, was $1, as they advertised in the Grants Pass newspaper. Burch discovers the Ghost Room.

1886   Harkness and Burch offer camping facilities near the cave for visitors. MacDanniels and Burch cut a trail from Williams Creek over Meadow Mountain,* cross Lake Creek to the caves from the northeast. A cabin was built sometime between 1886 and 1888 but the site of the cabin apparently was not recorded.

1888-?   Frank N. Nickerson and A. J. Henderson "took possession" of the cave and started Oregon Caves Improvement Company. However, the year 1894 might be more accurate as Steel said the Harkness brothers were guides in 1888.

1889   The Harkness Company folded. The venture proved unsuccessful in part because the nearest railroad was miles away and the southwestern Oregon area was sparsely populated. Homer Harkness left for Washington [*sic.*].

1890   Elijah Davidson took his 14-year old son into the cave. For the next few years, is was common for nearly everyone to break off a stalactite to take home as a souvenir.

---

* Meadow Mountain does not appear in popular reference sources or on the map of the Siskiyou National Forest, or in the U.S. Geological Survey *Geographic Names Information System - Oregon.*

194

There is an unauthenticated story that is reported to have been printed in the *Oregonian* in the mid-1930's. This was about some miners who came from California and claim to have found the caves. Believing that the cave formations were worth owning, they posted markers and measured for homesteads. When they arrived at the Land Office to file their claims, they were told the property was in Oregon and not in California. Rather than become Oregonians, the men disgustedly abandoned their claim.

1891   A "Captain" A. J. Smith of San Diego, California, W. J. Henderson, and F. M. Nickerson, held a mineral claim on the cave.

The *Examiner* sponsored a well-publicized expedition to assist with full-scale development. Reporter Charles Michelson and a photographer, Mr. Worthington, and apparently a staff artist, first went to Grants Pass by train then to Kerby by stagecoach. About four miles below the mouth of the canyon (shortly beyond the confluence of Sucker Creek with Grayback Creek), the party left the wagons and made up a pack train. (Most earlier parties seem to have approached the cave from Williams to the east. This trip is from the west.) They axed their way though the woods as no one appeared to have been over the trail for about two years – *see* Chapter 2.

The Oregon Caves Improvement Company's superintendent, Captain Smith, promoted a 500-room hotel with electric lighting, as well as a street car line from Grants Pass to the cave.

1892   C. J. Kincaid signed and dated a formation in the cave.

1894   Captain A. J. Smith secured a bond from Nickerson and his partners, employed surveyors to lay out a road and trails, hire men to explore and develop the cavern further, purchase supplies and install entrance gates. Apparently two cabins were built, one of a single story and the other two story near the cave entrance. A cabin was built on Sucker Creek, the place being called Camp Henderson. Between February and October, rubble was cleared to make paths in the caves and stalactites were broken to open passages (USFS 1924). Watson, writing in 1909 states that the "Captain" never entered the cave.

A second exploring party from the *Examiner* visited the cave as guests of the Oregon Cave Improvement Company. A special cabin was prepared for the occasion. Men of the *Examiner* crew began blasting inside the cave to open passages – *see* Chapter 2.

Even with the free publicity in the San Francisco newspaper, the cave was too remote therefore within months the company went into receivership. When the liabilities amounted to several thousand dollars, "Captain" Smith is said to have disappeared. At Sheriff's auction, the company's property realized just $60. John H. Kincaid and Nickerson continued as cave guides at least until 1909.

As there were so few visitors to be guided through the caves, Nickerson, an educated man, worked as a private teacher from his house in Kerby and also served as the county clerk when the Josephine County seat was in Kerby.

1896   The Grants Pass - Crescent City Stage Company advertised that it will carry parties of eight or more to the caves and return for a total of $7. Meals and lodging can be had along the way for 25¢ each person. The parties camp in the woods near the caves two or more days.

> **In September 1896, members of the National Forestry Commission are in the vicinity to study then make recommendations about what to do with public forest land both in and outside the established forest reserves. The group includes John Muir, Charles Sargent and Gifford Pinchot.**
>
> **The report is finished by February 1897 but Pinchot publishes a dissenting view for distribution to Congress. President Cleveland makes significant additions to the number and acreage of Forest Reserves. Some months later, the "Organic Act" is passed for the Forest Reserves, the legislation more in line with Pinchot's thinking than with the others of the commission. The first forest rangers are hired to protect the reserves from fire and timber poaching. This is important to the Oregon Caves as the monument is within the Forest Reserve.**

1901-?   Proctor, a writer of about 1915, combined the *Examiner's* and Smith's interests into a single venture stating this took place in 1901. William Randolph Hearst, the main financial backer and publisher of the *Examiner*, was said to have asked Smith to pay off the debt but Smith died soon after. Little of this account accords with other sources. The *Examiner's* group cleared land below the entrance to the cave and graded a road of several hundred feet along the east side of Cave Creek in the early 1900's – or was this in 1894?. (The creek, in 1888, known as Logan Creek, was renamed Cave Creek in 1913.)

196

1902   Henry Gannett, presents the fourth U. S. Geological Survey professional paper, *The Forests of Oregon*. The paper lays the groundwork for the reservation of future national forests. Crater Lake National Park is established from the Cascade Range Forest Reserve.

Due to land fraud trials in Oregon, President Roosevelt temporarily withdraws ten million acres of forest land from settlement and land claims. Included is land proposed for the Southern Oregon Forest Reserve. This prevents the Oregon Caves from being claimed under the mineral laws. Of potential detriment to the cave, if the Southern Oregon Forest Reserve is proclaimed, opponents claim, would be the halt of railroad development through the forest on its way to Crescent City. Among other opposing arguments were proponents of the California & Oregon Coast Railroad that the railroad was needed to bring tourists to the cave. The Grants Pass *Courier* editorialized on May 30, 1903, that a Forest Reserve would "kill our lumbering industry and cripple mining to such an extent that Southern Oregon would never recover [if] the reserve be made permanent."*

1905   The Forest Reserves are transferred from the Interior Department's General Land Office to the Department of Agriculture on February 1. Gifford Pinchot is named Chief Forester.

1906   The Siskiyou Forest Reserve is established. This allows certain mining and settlement to occur.

On June 8, Congress passes the Antiquities Act authorizing the president to proclaim national monuments with a proviso that "the limits of which in all cases shall be confined to the smallest area compatible with the proper care and management of the object [of antiquity]." The Act includes "...historic landmarks, historic and prehistoric structures and other objects of historic or scientific interest that are situated upon lands owned or controlled by the Government of the United States.

1907   Four sections, including the land on which the caves are located, were withdrawn on August 12 from all forms of entry including mining, for a "proposed" National Monument. Robert

---

*Attributed to The Rogue River *Courier* (no date). According to Turnbull's *History of Oregon Newspapers* (p.414) *The Daily Courier* of Grants Pass carried the name the *Rogue River Courier* for a number of years but to avoid confusion, was changed to the *Grants Pass Courier* when the town of Woodville changed its name to Rogue River in 1912. The Rogue River runs alongside both towns which are about eleven miles apart.

This cave decoration reminds some of Multnomah Falls on the Columbia River.

Veach attempted to locate a mineral claim on the cave area. When informed of the withdrawal of the land from mineral claims to the Forest Service, he and partner G. O. Ouim, applied for a special use permit to develop a cave resort. A newspaper is reported to have stated "Every citizen of this country is vitally interested in having the Oregon Caves exploited to the fullest extent."

Poet laureate of the Sierras, Joaquin Miller, with Chandler B. Watson, along with John Kincaid, make a special investigatory tour of the caves guided by Frank Nickerson. When Nickerson became "disoriented" (lost) Kincaid's dog, which had been left outside, suddenly appeared then showed the stranded party a new way to the outside from Paradise Lost.

1908   Ouim continued to apply for a Special Use Permit for the cave. Based on the policy of not allowing commercial monopolies on Forest Service lands, H. V. Anderson's Special Use Permit was not approved. The area was surveyed in October. When Siskiyou National Forest was created (1908), it was determined that the Oregon Caves are "very much mutilated" so said a Forest Service Report.

Map shows the only trails leading to the Monument: what is now known as the Nine Mile Oregon Caves Trail from Williams, which connected with the north end of what is now known as Big Tree Trail near what will later be the northern boundary of the Monument. There was also a second trail leading down Cave Creek toward the present city of Cave Junction.

Regrettable Incident

Frank Ellis, 21, his wife of three months, and a number of friends, visited the cave on August 2. Having become suspicious of two strangers who were in the cave when the party arrived, Ellis hand-carried his revolver. While climbing a ladder in the Beehive Room, he slipped and fell; his revolver hit the wall and fired. The bullet entered Ellis' left eye and brain. The group cried "murder" and everyone except Frank Ellis' wife fled the cave taking all the torches with them. He died shortly afterward. She followed the guide string to find her way out of the cave.

—"A Terrible Tragedy in Depths of Oregon Caves; Frank Ellis ... is Accidentally Killed." in *Courier*. [Grants Pass, Ore.] Aug. 6, 1909. p.1.

Due to this incident, as well as vandalism, the Forest Service decided that all persons entering the caves must have an official guide. In 1911, guide service started and continues to the present time. —Editor

---

1909   The year saw 360 visitors to the cave. The National Monument was established on July 12 (Proclamation No. 879). President Taft's proclamation states, "Any use of the land which interferes with its preservation or protection as a National Monument is hereby forbidden." The monument is to be administered by the U. S. Forest Service. According to Carter Davidson's daughter, Elijah was upset about misinformation concerning his finding of the cave and would have nothing to do with the monument's operations. By now, the single story cabin had had its floor, door and part of the roof ripped off as fuel for campfires. The two-story cabin had also been vandalized.

"The Craggies (*sic.*) Caves on the Applegate [river] Drainage was also in the running for Monument status but they were 'not opened properly' and so lost out." *

1910   Grazing allotments in national forest land had been delineated along Sucker Creek and Grayback Creek by this time. Dick Rowley leads 367 visitors through the caves.

1911   About 90 percent of people visiting the cave came from the Williams Creek side and most of them arrived on foot. An automobile dirt road, to the head of Williams Creek is "in fair condition." The sum of $500 was spent for construction of 2½ miles of new trail at the cave end of the trail from Williams Creek and on replacing 35 wooden ladders in the cave. Ladders made of wood last about two years. A small log store house for tools is constructed by the cave guide 525 feet below the caves to house equipment when not in use. Tents house the guide, his wife and their 10-year-old boy. A railroad** was started from Grants Pass with Crescent City to be its western terminal. The railroad, which would offer connections with Southern Pacific in Grants Pass, would bring thousands of visitors to the cave, promoters hawked, but hard times hit and the track and was never built beyond Waters Creek on Highway 199. During the year, Watson inquired about a use permit for a resort facility for the cave. T. H. Johnson applied for a Special Use Permit to light the caves.

1911   Forest Service employs guides to provide free tours and to protect the caves between July 1 and October 1. Dick Rowley, Vick-

---

* Attributed to National Park Service official "TIMELINE" of events concerning the Oregon Caves. Formal name is "Lower Craggy Cave," according to U.S. Forest Service. This is a "wild cave" and is a closed federally protected site – a "sensitive" area.

** The sad tale of the California & Oregon Coast Railroad is detailed in *The Siskiyou Line, Adventure in Railroading*. Refer to bibliography.

ers Smith, and Richard Sowell, get the jobs. They spend part of their time improving trails at the caves.

(EDITOR'S NOTE: The guide service at the Oregon Caves was established one year before the first naturalist (guide) in the National Park system began work at Mount Rainier National Park.

1912　　A Portland group announced plans to build a road to the caves as well as an hotel. Mrs. Ethel Sowell held a Special Use Permit for the Government Camp just outside the monument boundary. This is thought to have been about 75 feet above the present lower parking lot. For many years Ethel and Dick Sowell guided parties up the trail from their Caves Camp on the Williams side of the mountain, then Dick Rowley guided these visitors through the caves. Ethel Sowell provided tent lodging and meals.

Senator Bourne agrees to push for National Park designation. Representative Hawley asks the Forest Service why certain permits for development have not been approved.

Anderson applies for a permit to hydroelectrically light the cave and to build a two-story log structure close to the present Chateau site. He also announced that private money is available to build a wagon road up the mountain from Sucker Creek.

A newspaper article promoting development complains of "seemingly unnecessary delay" and "red tape" from the government. A permit for T. H. Johnston to provide cave guides, light the caves and maintain safe ladders in the caves is typed but never dated or signed.

The Department of Agriculture lawyer renders an opinion that the Forest Service has no authority to issue a permit for building a hotel on a National Monument (Graves, 1912). Representatives of the War, Interior and Agriculture Departments meet to decide that the Oregon Caves National Monument should not be developed and managed by private parties even under departmental restrictions (Adams 1912).

Attorney Shaw advised that the National Park [or] the Forest Service should not be authorized to grant the desired concessions. Anderson circulates a petition to have Oregon Caves changed to a National Park.

An automobile road is completed from Grants Pass to Holland, some fifteen miles west of the caves.

1913   A local group (Game and Fish Protective Association) pushes for a 200,000 acre National Park to facilitate building a road and a hotel. Senator Bourne and Congressman Hawley each introduce bills in Congress to change the National Monument to National Park status. The Bourne bill provides for mining and for permits by restaurant and hotel keepers but not for economic monopolies.

The Bourne increase in acreage (36 square miles) proposal is opposed because the "caves are small and disappointing to most visitors" and it would prohibit timber sales and grazing. The Hawley bill requests 240 acres and allows for timber sales and grazing. This bill is supported by Forester Graves (Grants Pass *Courier* Dec 12, 1913).

The head of the Forest Service intends to ask Congress for authority to grant permits for hotel and other purposes in the Siskiyou National Forest and then revoke National Monument status so it would again be a part of Siskiyou National Forest. He is anxious for such development as development of timber "is still some ways off" in Siskiyou National Forest. He feels it would be difficult to have a National Park enacted because of the large number of such requests for National Parks in the west. His plan is approved by the Grants Pass Commercial Club.*

An automobile road up the Applegate Valley leads to Steven's Ranch, with a ten mile hike to the caves. Camping tents and bedding were intermittently provided at the ranch by the Grants Pass Commercial Club from at least 1913 to 1917 (*Argus,* June 10, 1915, McDuff, 1917). The total cost from Portland including rail-road fare to Grants Pass was about $18.

Davidson leads a group of Mazamas (a mountaineering club from Portland that Steel founded in 1894) through the cave on his last reported cave guiding trip. The Mazamas call the cave the "Oregon Mammoth Caves."

Ira Sparlin chips away formations to allow some tourists access to some of the rooms.

1914   Government guides, Dick Rowley and D. B. Reynolds give three to four trips per day through the caves although their contract says they only have to provide one trip a day.

1915   An Act in 1915 authorized lease of Forest Service lands for hotels, summer resorts and other recreational uses but the Forest

---

* "Commercial Club" was an early name for Chambers of Commerce.

Service decides not to grant any permits for the cave until an automobile road reaches the monument.

1916   Dick Rowley says that Lerman notified him that concessions would not be granted within the National Monument. This is denied by Lerman. The secretary of Agriculture says, "It is our policy to encourage the development of recreation areas, like the Oregon Caves, in every way possible." (Houston 1917). The District Forester believed that Grants Pass developers "are entitled to some voice in fixing the conditions for permits (Cecil, 1917).

> A telephone at the cave works poorly because the telephone is connected at the end of an overloaded "farmer" line. The line was a turn-the-crank "magneto" party line to a switchboard believed to have been in Kerby.

1917   C. W. Howland, Dick Rowley's brother-in-law, began furnishing accommodations for tourists at Caves Camp (Lain, 1917). Saddle and pack horses were furnished upon advance notice. Mules, horses and foot-power carried people up the last steep ten miles to the caves – a rugged hike for some.

Meals at the end of the Williams Road were fifty cents. Tents for two rented for $1.25 and mules could be hired for $2.50 each, according to an article in the *Sunday Oregonian.*

1920   During the year 1,800 visitors traveled ten miles by trail from the Williams Valley via Stevens Ranch, or eight miles by trail from the Holland Valley via Grimmit's Ranch.

Two toilets and a small terrace built by Dick Rowley on a level with the main entrance and used for a stable and temporary camps are now in use. Rowley surveys part of the cave.

1920   Automobile made it to within 1½ miles of the caves in May. Road officially opened on June 26. Only 50 cars were allowed on the highway at one time to prevent congestion. The parking loop at the caves had room for between 20 and 30 automobiles. The 11.7 mile road along with the required bridge over Cave Creek cost $295,000 to construct.

1922   McIlveen ran a tent camp and provided food at the cave under the first contract granted by the Forest Service. Meals were 75¢ and $1. Two-person size tents were rented for $1 per night. Carbide lamps rented for 15¢ and coveralls for 35¢ were also available. The mess tent was on the present Chalet site.

"The Oregon Cavemen" was founded to publicize Grants Pass and the Oregon Caves. In 1936, 8-year old movie star Shirley Temple visited the "Cavemen." This young actress captured the hearts of the public in several pictures. In 1934, the Academy gave her a special "Oscar" in grateful recognition for her outstanding contribution to screen entertainment. At 21, she retired from movie making.

Dick Rowley and J. H. Campbell open stream passage from Ghost Room and another passage running in the general direction of the main galleries, together several hundred feet long. Most hands-and-knees crawlways along main route are now eliminated.

Senator Stanfield introduces bill in Congress to light the caves and provide shelter for visitors.

The Assistant District Forester says that "the administration of the Service will be judged largely by the character of the service rendered by the permittee. It is therefore very much to our interest to see that the proper services are required and rendered."

Lighting of the caves should be done either by the Forest Service or by some public body rather than by a concessionaire who would then have a legitimate proprietary interest in the caves and the cave's improvements.

> **Visitor is reprimanded for breaking formations on September 16. District Forester Cecil says visitors are defacing cave walls with carbide lamps and urges electrification to put an end to this vandalism.** —*Coquille Valley Sentinel*

A new road is built between Grants Pass and Crescent City. New route is six miles shorter than former route by way of Holland. A gravel road one lane wide (8-feet) to the cave from the Redwood Highway is completed in December but not officially opened until June of 1922. To get a steam shovel to the cave area, the road is widened to 14-feet.

A volunteer group of Grants Pass businessmen called "The Oregon Cavemen," incorporate to publicize Grants Pass and the caves. The Cavemen held a ceremony in the caves and regularly appear at public gatherings "kidnapping politicians and pretty women."

In 1921, about 1,900 people visit the cave area but not all enter the caves.

1923   The Forest Service granted a concession to the Oregon Caves Company, a corporation of ten Grants Pass businessmen, including Amos E. Voorhies, the publisher of the *Courier*. The company built the Chalet (guide headquarters) for about $5,000 and took over the guide service. The northeast side of the Chalet holds a dining room and kitchen. The southwest side has a store, office, storeroom and restroom with running water. The sewage field empties right into the head of stream. Four tents houses for visitors are above the Chalet. Latrines are on both sides of the ravine.

A summer resort, including store, is to be at the mouth of Grayback Creek. Because the Chalet and sewage system cost more than anticipated, the company successfully asks Forest Service to allow it to delay development there. Company agrees to repair broken formations in the caves caused by visitors on tours. The company asks for the right to maintain a tennis court, bowling alleys, pool tables and other "sources of amusement." Even after spending $6,000 in improvements, the company nets a profit of $2,000 in gross receipts.

Grayback Campground cost $998 to develop. The Lind-home resort provides board, lodging, a store and gasoline one-half mile from the monument .

Dick Rowley finished replacing wooden stairs with steel stairs.

Connecting road from main highway (No. 199), closed due to winter snows, becomes passable by late April. 10,000 people visit the cave. Latrines established at caves.

Approval of a permit for guide service and to construct a lunch room is delayed by the Forest Service for two months on the conjecture that the Crater Lake National Park concessionaire wants to add an Oregon Caves operation to his string of hotels.

In April, concessionaire (Sabin's Oregon Caves Company – with a 20 year contract) obtains the services of landscape engineer Professor Arthur L. Peck of the Oregon Agricultural College. Peck recommends that a substantial building be placed on the site of the present Chalet and that it should be an "alpine" type because it should be picturesque and distinctive. It is to have a sheathing of Port Orford cedar bark because of the attractive way that bark weathers and blends with the surroundings.

1924   A small parking lot is built right south of the caves as overnight guests object to leaving their cars 900 feet away in the large regular parking lot then having to walk and lug their suit-cases on the trail to the Chalet. Due to crowding, camping is no longer permitted in the parking lot.

During the summer, Sabin and Rowley discovered the Big Tree, a Douglas fir nearly thirteen feet diameter and about 160 feet tall. It is the largest tree of its type in Oregon.

On July 30, the United States Post Office Department noting a need by concessionaire and resident employees, opened a

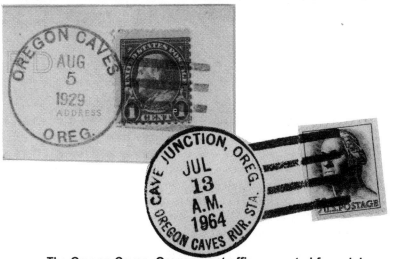

The Oregon Caves, Oregon post office operated from July 30, 1924 through March 31, 1956 as a summer-only (16 June - 16 September) office. It became Oregon Caves Rural Station of Cave Junction, Oregon but was discontinued on September 16, 1977.

summer only post office at the caves. George C. Sabin was named first postmaster. In 1998, the federal and concessionaire facilities are served by the postal service's rural route as well as by United Parcel Service and Federal Express.

1925 Cabins and electric light plant built. Cabins have running water. The power plant is just above the northeast end of the Chalet. Electricity installed in buildings, cottages and tent houses which were increased to ten. Lights hung on trees. Lunches and dinners served to members of Home Economics Department visitors from Oregon Agricultural College at Corvallis. A nursery is provided for children too small to make the cave trip.

A cumulative total of $372 has been spend on widening passages and $4,392 on cave trails and ladders. It cost $63,489.25 for the Forest Service to operate the Monument.

1926 A hard surface was put on the Caves Highway from town to milepost 6. Seven cabins, a guide shack (studio), a guide dormitory situated above the large parking lot, and a road about 500 feet long south of the caves are built. The studio is used to store lanterns and other equipment.

To keep stream water clean, the septic field is carried around the hill to where the old carbide house once stood. Several obsolete and "objectionable" buildings are removed.

Net profits eliminated close to half of the $10,000 concession debt.

Town of Cave Junction established. (Does not get its post office until 1936.)

1927   The Caves Highway was widened to eighteen feet, repairs and gravel added to most areas. The Grants Pass *Courier* declared on May 6th that "all dangerous curves are being eliminated."

The concession can house 56 people. The guide headquarters can house 14 and now has flush toilets.

There is concern for fire wood as the supply of dead timber is nearly exhausted. Trees classed as "part defective" and least desirable for marketing, are cut for firewood.

1928   A gasoline and carbide heating system is installed in the rental cabins.

1929   Congress appropriated $35,000 for the construction of an exit tunnel, cave lighting and cave water pipes.

The Forest Service proposes to divert a portion of guide fees to maintenance of the cave. The Forest Service surveys part of the cave yielding 1,860 feet.

1930   The Nepage-McKenny Company of Portland won a bid at $22,521 to install lights in the cave. This included three miles of wire and 30 switches for 180 lights. These were: 134 50 watt, 36 100 and 200 watt and 10 500 watt bulbs. Power is from an 80 horsepower diesel engine. "The specification for the cable (conductor) and the outlet boxes will be drawn in such a way that the job will be permanent for all times." [*sic.*]

Water pipe was installed in the cave and a shelter (shack) for the standby generator is built.

The concessionaire argues that the cave development (lighting and water) will increase its costs. Senator McNary opposes asking the concession to maintain cave developments and feels the fees should be lowered so as not to allow the concession to "profit unduly by reasons of outlay of federal funds."

A 1.3 mile trail is built to Big Tree.

1931   Caves Highway becomes fully paved and widened with 25 men working on this for several months. A service station in the large parking lot is in operation.

The Associate Forester states that reducing guide fees "would have a cheapening effect." He argues that the government and the concession should evenly split profits from a monopoly permit which the concessionaire holds.

> The Oregon Caves was one of the few National Monuments that experienced any concession development prior to 1933. This presented some unique challenges to the National Park Service when it assumed jurisdiction due to the preexisting concession operation. In addition was the fact that when compared to its other properties, the Oregon Caves National Monument presented a fierce task due to its steep topography and small size.

The new 20-year hotel permit charges the concession $100 per year and allows the concession to change the proposed site of the lodge (Chateau). The separate Special Use Permit authorizing the concession to furnish guide service can be terminated at any time by the Forest Service.

The concessionaire is charged fifty percent of net profits from tour fees.

1932   Lunch and dinners now cost $1.00. Breakfast is 50¢. An art studio at the caves has probably (?) now been established.

1933   The timber for the lodge (Chateau) was cut, taken from an island in the middle of Sucker Creek by the Baldwin ranch and hauled to a mill by truck. The Villair and Anderson Mill on Caves Highway at milepost 14 milled the lumber. The cedar bark siding was taken from a railroad tie cutting operation on Grayback Creek near Grayback Camp.

During construction, carpenters become snowed in. When they complained they were told that, being carpenters, they could build skis. They did and skied out.

A Forest Service patrolman, paid $400 per year, patrols, cares for and maintains campgrounds 100 days each year when he is not called to fight forest fires. A District Ranger makes inspections of campgrounds and caves for less than $150 annually. Administration of the monument costs about $700 per year. On June 10, a Federal Executive Order transfers administration of Oregon Caves from the U. S. Forest Service to the National Park Service.

1934   The six story lodge (Chateau) is completed. Total cost is $50,000. Construction plans started in 1929. Stock was sold to finance the project. The Chateau is steam heated. Madrone balusters support a fir handrail. The ballroom has a maple floor and the fireplace on the fourth floor (lobby level) is of marble salvaged from blasting during construction. A stream (Cave Creek) runs through the third floor dining room and is crossed by two bridges.

Steak dinners are $1. Chicken dinner is 75¢. Breakfast is 35¢ to 60¢. Lodging, offered all year, for two ranges from $2.25 to $8 per night. Rental of a cottage is $2.50 per night.

The offices in the Chalet have now been moved to the northeast side and a two-story restroom has been built at the large parking lot. The cabins are now electrically heated.

Oregon Caves, and $165,446 of Forest Service developments and improvements, is transferred to the National Parks Service on April 1, 1934

Park Ranger Finch is told not to interfere with what is being done. He records, "Everything connected with the Chateau is organized and under the management of Mr. Sabin" (concession manager). Many powerful institutions are determined to keep the overall operation as it has been although the National Park Service Director tells Finch to start an "agitation" in Grants Pass for the enlargement of the Monument, but to stay in the background until the agitation reaches the "point of being a demand of the people." Mr. Harvey Grant of the Grants Pass Chamber of Commerce is contacted.

The proposed creation of a National Park, sponsored by park concessionaires and other locals would include Bolan Lake which is on the east slope of Grayback Mountain.

The ranger feels he has "no particular niche to fill." He cheerily greets every visitor entering the Monument five days a week. He also gives campfire "speeches" to visitors and to the CCC boys from the nearby CCC camp.

> **Over 20 percent of people entering the National Monument do not visit the caves. Only 11 percent of all visitors are not from Oregon or California.**

Some of the 266 feet of 2,300 volt power lines crossing the cave trail show signs of wear. Finch recommends the lines be encased in concrete conduit under the trail.

Cattle graze over the Monument and is of concern to some visitors.

1935   (On an undetermined date but after 1934, emergency telephones were installed in the caves.) The Forest Service rules to share concession profits enhanced by government activities at the Monument. The *Oregonian* (Portland) on June 25th editorialized that the concession would operate at a loss if it had to pay 50 percent of the guide service profits to the government, as visitation and use of the lodge decreased during the Great Depression. The National Park Service negotiates a 15-year single contract with the concession that covers all its operations. The NPS contract revokes the Forest Service permits.

The highway between Cave Junction and Grants Pass is as twisted as the road from Cave Junction to the Monument.

1936   Town of Cave Junction received a post office on May 11. The post office postmarked its own mail until recent large volumes of mail, nationally, causes nearly all outgoing mail from small post offices to be trucked to a postal Sectional Center for processing. Most mail from Cave Junction is postmarked in Medford, 84 miles away.

1937   Private contractors, that started the Exit Tunnel in 1933, were unable to complete the job. The government, with its CCC projects, completed the work. This eliminates the need for tour groups to double-back to the "110-Exit" to leave the caves. When Exit Tunnel is opened for public use the typical cave tour of 2 to 2½ hours is reduced to 1¼ hours.

1938   The caves are lighted now by commercial power from the sub-station at Holland, Oregon, east of Cave Junction. The wires are on poles through the forest. The lines going into the cave are in non-metallic, armored cable. The diesel power plant is reconditioned for standby service. 200 high-wattage lights are added to caves with lights every 60 feet in the Exit Tunnel. Exterior lights in the Monument are close to the ground for summer season and lamps high on poles for winter season.

1939   The first mention of algae growing in the caves, near light bulbs is mentioned. Daily contact between the Monument and Crater Lake National Park is by short-wave radio.

1940   Rangers give campfire programs on summer evenings in front of caves.

1941   The landing field south of Cave Junction is completed by men from Oregon Caves CCC. Runway will handle DC-3 transports. Listed on aeronautical charts as emergency field during World War-II, later became Forest Service smoke-jumper training base.

1942   Chalet is rebuilt, 3rd floor added and north wing lengthened. The public contact and rest rooms at the end of the large parking lot is built at cost of $5,000. The guide dormitory is remodeled. The guide shack (also called "studio" or lamp storage house) is dismantled. It had been used by guides for rests between tours.

Richard Sabin, nephew of George Sabin, is now General Manager of the concession.

Crater Lake Natural History Association established to support educational and interpretative programs at Crater Lake, Lava Beds and Oregon Caves.

1943-1944   Due to gasoline and tire rationing as a result of the war effort, visits drop to fewer than 4,000 per year.

1944   A new concession contract is approved.

1945   A Congressional Committee on Claims, recommends that the concession only pay those fees for 1934 and 1935 that would have been required if the 1936 contract had been in force—the fee $100 per year. A bill to this effect is passed by Congress.

1946   Cave lighting system is overhauled and improved.

1949   Guide dormitory appraised at $9,124, the National Park Service quarters at $6,000, auto and tool storage shed at $600, the seven cabins at $4.679.07. The lodge (Chateau) quadruples in value from its original cost. The Chalet is valued at $64,778.66.

1951   National Park Service and Forest Service agree that Oregon Caves boundary be extended from 480 acres to 2,910 acres. Josephine County Court supports the expansion. Never implemented. Forest Service terminates its agreement in 1959.

1952   Ranger gives talks of about five minutes duration at evening campfires in front of the lodge (Chateau). No permanent Interpretative Rangers are at the Monument.

The concession operates the Chalet as a ticket office for tours, curio shop, soda fountain, nursery and dressing room. The two upper floors provide dormitory quarters for female employees.

1953   Section of main parking area begins to sluff off due to erosion. (Occurs again in 1997 forcing closure of historic Ranger Station. New offices built on opposite side of main parking lot.)

1954   Dick Rowley, 84, retires after 42 years at Oregon Caves.

1955   A bill is introduced in the U.S. House of Representatives to expand the Monument to include its water supply source. The bill fails. Gates are installed on all cave entrances.

1957   Cave lights overhauled and improved. The tour path in the caves is covered with asphalt.

1958   A bill is reintroduced in the House of Representatives to expand the Monument to include its water supply. The bill again fails to pass.

Dick Rowley, now age 89, guides a cave tour.

Bats, while attempting to navigate between the spaces in the gate, became entangled in the metal bar angles where the bats died. Filling the angles with silicone rubber was done in an attempt to ease the bats' passage.

1959   William Halliday's group begins comprehensive survey of the caves.

Women concession employees start providing cave tours.

1960   Ladder running from Ghost Room floor to top of the breakdown was replaced with stairs. Exit trail is paved. Average number of visitors per vehicle is 3.7.

1961   The diesel generator is sold. Sharp rocks in cave ceilings of low passageways are removed or smoothed throughout the cave.

1962   The spiral stairs in cave are installed. A lady visitor, 102 years of age, tours cave.

1963   Corps of Engineers designated the caves as fallout shelter in event of nuclear attack but Superintendent of Crater Lake, and Speleologist Holliday casts doubt on effective use of the cave as fallout shelter.

1964   Early cave guide Dick Rowley died at age 95.

The infamous Christmas 1964 flood inundates the Chalet and Chateau. Flood waters swamp the Chalet gift shop. In the lodge, the first three floors are severely damaged. Estimated damage to concession property is $100,000.

A young guide placed the concession manager's wife in a snow plow as the waters rose. He panicked and left the plow.

When the woman tried to free herself, she was swept under the plow where she lodged. The guide then went back to the plow and helped her to safety. She was injured but not severely.

William Halliday's survey party completed the mapping work showing about 7,500 feet of passages.

Late 1960's Colored lights phased out except in Paradise Lost. The old CCC automobile and storage shed is dismantled.

1965 Lodging charges at the Chateau range between $6.50 single room to $21 for suites.

1966 Lower parking lot is enlarged. Will now hold 108 cars. Visitors with trailers are to leave trailers in Cave Junction due to limited space in the Monument and no satisfactory way of turning a long-hauler when the lot is congested with cars.

1968 The one millionth visitor goes through the caves.

1969 Study reveals that the Monument contributes $3 million tourism dollars to the surrounding area annually (*Herald and News*, Sept. 14).

Starting July 1, Monument no longer administered by Crater Lake National Park.

1970 It is observed that visitors are encouraged to rent rubber raincoats and galoshes from the concessionaire to protect street clothing and footwear.

1971 The Bureau of Land Management rules that a marble mining claim about half-mile from the Monument is invalid, based on withdrawal of four sections of land around the cave in 1907 from use of all kinds under the Public Land Laws – including Mineral Laws.

Tempest between concession employees and NPS management brings short walkout then slow-down of workers with report to Equal Employment Opportunity Commission. Backups and delays everywhere; visitors had long waits for cave tours, and guests got great two hour tours that day.

A resurvey of the caves 7,400 feet of passages to date.

1972 Mineral rights are withdrawn (Public land Order No. 5,226) outside the original four sections withdrawn earlier to protect potable water source.

1973 Cave tour route repaved.

1974 Metal stairs replaced in the Imagination Room, Limbo

Rock, Paradise Lost and above and immediately below the Bird of Paradise.

1976   Spotlight in Ghost Room moved from the breakdown top by Angel Falls to the Ghost Room Terrace. Fluorescent lamps installed in cave. The shed for the standby generator is dismantled.

National Park Service proposes a Visitor's Center be located in Cave Junction.

1978   Boundary change (Public Law 95-625) authorizes approximately eight acres in City of Cave Junction for proposed Oregon Caves Tourist Reception Center. Area later reduced to four acres.

1982   The Lost Caves Timber Sale is approved in exchange for a fire escape road that will be used to haul timber out of the area north of the Monument. Small forest fires in the vicinity of the caves had occurred in past but there was never before a fire escape route from the Monument.

1983   Third millionth visitor goes through caves.

1984   Subterranean telephone cable from Cave Junction to Monument installed.

1985   Chateau rates change from $39 to $44 double. Cave tour rates are $4.50 for adults and $2.50 for children.

Cave management returned to control of Superintendent of Crater Lake National Park.

1986   Removal of construction rubble earlier dumped in crevices in cave begins. About 10,000 square feet of cave is opened for the first time in about fifty years.

1987   Three culverts diverting the River Styx and 64 cubic yards of construction rubble were removed from cave. The CCC may have installed these culverts in 1935.

1988   205 cubic yards of construction rubble removed from cave. All cabins over the cave, except one (to be used as an office), dismantled. The cave tour fee is $5.75 for adults and $3.00 for children.

The concessionaire is charged fifty percent of net profits from tour fees.

1989   Except for a few sections of paved trail, most of the area between the Main Entrance and the Spiral Stairs is restored.

Historic cabins built on top of the cave were removed (except for one) when a broken water pipe caused flooding in cave's Passageway of the Whale.

1990   A new style gate with horizontal bars is installed on the 110 Exit to better allow bats to get through the gate.

Substantial modifications have occurred that have affected the airflow in the Oregon Caves. The Connecting Tunnel and Exit Tunnel were blasted, and the Icebox Cave entrance was closed in the 1930's. In the 1950's some passages were enlarged and some were blocked including entrance to the Carbide Room. These operations affect relative humidity, temperature, carbon dioxide levels, condensation corrosion ("acid dew") all have some affect on cave life. To restore airflow patterns, the National Park Service began restoring the original size of passages both in the cave and at entrances. Two airlocks were installed and the entrance to the Carbide Room was reopened.

The temperature at the Monument reaches –8 degrees F.

New Visitor's Center opens in Cave Junction.

1991   A natural entrance is restored to original size and a bat gate installed.

1992   The asphalt pavement was removed due to petroleum, a component of asphalt, leaching into the cave. Paths repaved with rough-surface concrete.

1993   Rules changed to permit children under six to caves but children must be at least 42-inches tall and show stamina by demonstrating ability to climb test stairs unassisted.

EARTHWATCH volunteers complete room-by-room inventory of the known cave and finish second year of mapping. About 1/3 of known cave is completed.

1994   Daycare is discontinued.

1995   Cave closed January 16 - February 28 to install first 300 feet of new trail starting at main entrance. Lighting is redesigned. Some lights can be turned off after guided tour passes a point to reduce algae where it is hard to reach with Clorox spraying.

Up to about a dozen bats start using the 110 bat gate. Up to twenty bats appear to be using new bat gate at cave's entrance. There are few historical accounts of bat usage of these areas.

Jaguar bones discovered off the Ghost Room. Bear bones, probably grizzly are radiocarbon dated at over 50,000 years old by far the oldest known grizzly in North America.

EARTHWATCH volunteers finish third year of mapping; about 2/3's of known cave has been completed.

1996   Ice Box Cave Entrance reopened.

1997   The Draft General Management Plan and Environmental Impact Statement, a 226 page report, for Oregon Caves National Monument is issued in December.

The caves were closed for renovation in December and in January and February 1998.

It was quite a job to build the Oregon Caves Highway.

The Oregon Caves Chateau

Appendix I
The Grand Chateau
A Wedding at the Oregon Caves

A look at the "Timeline" for activities at the Oregon Caves will reveal there were at the least, thoughts about building a hotel nearby from very earliest times.

Harkness and Burch built a shake-covered shack in 1885. In 1887 the Oregon Caves Improvement Company fancied itself as the proprietor-operator of a hotel but there was no road to bring people to the caves. With few visitors and no cash backup system in place, the firm folded.

It would be 1922 before a suitable road was in place. The next year, the U. S. Forest Service granted a 20-year concession to the Oregon Caves Company which had been formed earlier as the Oregon Caves Resort, for the purpose of development of the caves and providing guide service. George Sabin was the General Manager. This corporation was founded by ten Grants Pass businessmen, including Amos E. Voorhies, the publisher of the *Courier*. The company built the Chalet to be a headquarters for the guides, at a cost of about $5,000 and took over the guide service. The northeast side of the Chalet held a dining room and kitchen. On the southwest side was a store, office, storeroom and restroom with running water.

Seeking an architect to design a hotel, the group interested Arthur L. Peak, a landscape engineer at Oregon Agricultural College in Corvallis, to become involved. Peak recommends that a substantial building be placed on the site of the present Chalet and that it should be an "alpine" type because it should be picturesque (rustic) and distinctive. The buildings would all be covered with a sheathing of Port Orford cedar bark because of the attractive way that bark weathers and blends with the surroundings.

Peak's plan was for an alpine village where he envisioned driveways between the various buildings and the cave entrance.

Due to complaints, a small parking lot was built just south of the caves entrance as overnight guests objected to leaving their cars 900 feet away in the large regular parking lot then having to lug their suit-

(TOP) The Chateau as it appeared in the mid-1930's.
(LOWER) Typical suite in the Chateau. Note the steam-heated radiator.

C - 14 625 Lounge - Oregon Caves Chateau

(TOP) The lounge and fireplace. The fine, polished floor was ruined in the Christmas 1964 flood and had to be taken up. It was replaced with plywood covered with fine wall-to-wall carpet. (LOWER) The fireplace is 2-sided.

C - 14 616 Fireplace - Oregon Caves Chateau

221

from Oregon Caves Chateau

(TOP) **Main stairway in the Chateau.** (LOWER) **The lodge appears as a 2½ story building from the road but from the bottom of the ravine, is 6 stories tall. Lower photograph made in March 1998.**

222

The Chateau in distance seen through the arch of the Chalet on a snowy day in March 1998.

cases on the trail to the Chalet. This secondary parking lot fit nicely into the overall plan. Because of an increase in the arrival of automobiles from town, camping was discontinued in the main parking lot.

Within a few years, after the present Redwood Highway (No. 199) was finished, seven cabins (then called "cottages") were constructed on the side of the mountain above the caves. Sam Baker, one of the incorporators of the concession, brought in Gust Lium, his brother-in-law, of Grants Pass, who was an excellent builder.

Lium listened carefully to Baker's ideas for a major hotel then Lium decided to place what would become a great monument in the crotch of the mountain just below the entrance to the caves. This ravine sported Cave Creek, the stream that flowed from the caves.

From the front, the building would appear only as two stories with tall steep dormers to shed the winter snow. From the opposite downstream (west) side, the lodge was a full six stories tall. All of this was "shoehorned" into the ravine. Work started in September of 1931 and by late spring of 1934 was ready for occupancy.

———

The Oregon Caves have always been a favorite place for Connie Baker who has loved the caves from the time of her first visit at age 3. She first toured the caverns in 1914. Then there was no paved road to the entrance so the last seven winding miles up the mountain were

223

traveled on horseback. For light in the cave, the parties carried candles. Then, as she was far too small to "do the course" – the hike in the caves – her first visit was on her father's shoulders. Sam Baker would become the concessionaire but that was years off.

Eventually, on June 23, 1934, Miss Constance Baker and Omar C ("Slug") Palmer were married in the Chateau. It was a big day at the Chateau for the construction was barely completed and this was the first semi-public event to be held there. The building would not open to the public for another month.

The Chateau was an "absolutely spectacular and rustic place nestled at the head of a steep valley lost in the mountains," gushed a contemporary reporter.

"In those days when you put on a wedding it was a family affair. You didn't have caterers or flower shops. Family members all pitched in to provide whatever was needed," Mrs. Palmer recalled nearly 65 years later.

Mr. and Mrs. Palmer revisit Chateau on 50th Anniversary.

The groom was part of the work party for he spent a day traipsing after his aunt who was in charge of the flowers, as she scoured the mountainside picking wild rhododendrons for decorations.

The time was in the heart of the depression and there was no photographer available, therefore there were no wedding pictures.

For the nuptials, 175 guests attended. The Bakers were from

The Chateau as it has been traditionally called, had its name changed to the "Lodge" in 1995. Picture made in March 1998.

Grants Pass, 50 miles away and the Palmer's traveled 300 miles from Portland.

As to accommodations for this crowd, Mrs. Palmer recalled that "My dad had taken all the rooms over for our out-of-town guests." The event was also a shakedown for the new kitchen and dining room.

Fifty years later, June 23, 1984, as part of their Golden Wedding Anniversary, the Palmer's revisited the Chateau.

The "Lodge" as the Chateau was renamed in 1995, is owned by the National Park Service but is managed by Oregon Caves Company, a subsidiary of The Estey Corporation.

The Chateau was listed on the *National Register of Historic Places* as an Historic Landmark May 28, 1987. ◇

The Palmers were interviewed for this book in spring 1998, "Slug" Palmer's 90th year.

—Editor

GLOSSARY

Air Lock In the Oregon Caves, metal doors inserted in passageways to prevent flow of unwanted air into the cave – air that can damage the cave's natural environment.

Bacon Thin sheet of *calcite* with alternating light and dark bands or stripes which resemble a strip of bacon. Dark bands may be caused by stain of iron oxide.

Bedding Plane A meeting (stratification) of two different layers of *sedimentary rock.*

Blade *Calcite* sheet one deposited in a crack but later exposed.

Breakdown Rubble on a cave floor caused by collapse of ceiling of a cavern or wall.

Calcium Bicarbonate Unstable compound occurring when *carbonic acid* comes in contact with calcium carbonate.

Calcium Carbonate Mineral. In chemistry: $CaCO_3$.

Calcite Crystalline form of calcium carbonate.

Carbonic Acid Weak acid. In chemistry H_2CO_3.

Clastic Dike Dike made of fragments of pre-existing rocks.

Column The growing together of a *stalagmite* and a *stalactite.*

Deposit Natural occurrence of mineral material. In cave jargon, any formation in a cave originating from deposition.

Drapery *Speleotherm* hanging in the form of a drapery or curtain.

Dripstone *Calcite* deposit caused by dripping water.

Flowstone *Calcite* deposit caused by flowing water across a cave floor or wall.

Fracture The general appearance of a broken surface of a mineral.

Gallery Subterranean passageway in a cave.

Ground Water Water in the earth as may be tapped with a well.

Helictite Form of *stalactite* other than which hangs vertically. May have side growths resembling twisted roots from vegetation.

Horizontal Gate Bars Gates at entry and exits of the cave that permit bats to fly between the bars compared with more common vertical gate bars that would not permit bats to pass.

Joint Crack, which in *limestone* forms at an angle to a *bedding plane.* Several joints may intersect each other as a four-sided pattern.

Air lock

Limestone Rock made mostly of *calcium carbonate*. Often an accumulation of organic remains as found in shells.

Marble Crystallized *limestone* caused by metamorphism (a change in the constitution of rock as a pronounced change effected by pressure, heat, and water, that results in a more compact and more highly crystalline condition).

Metamorphose To change into a different form – striking make over as change from *limestone* (sedimentary rock) to *marble* (metamorphic rock).

Moonmilk (Mondmilch) Rare form of hydromagnesite or *calcium carbonate* in a semisolid state.

110 Exit Earlier knows as the "upper" entrance, this orifice is 110 feet higher elevation than the cave entrance. It is 784-feet from the lower entrance by way of the cave tour.

Phreatic Zone Region below water table where rock is saturated with water (H_2O)

Plutonic (geology) Formed far below the surface of the earth by intense heat, great pressure and slow cooling. Plutonic rocks are typically crystalline and granitelike.

Popcorn Nodules of mineral deposits formed to resemble popcorn.

Rimstone *Calcite* deposit along the edge of a pool of water often in a cavern. Often appears as a somewhat lump of rock.

River Styx In Oregon Caves, the icy river (creek) that flows through lower reaches of the cave. It originates outside the cave.

Sedimentary Rock Made of *deposits* of sediments or from other minerals.

Shale *Sedimentary rock* made of clay or silt.

Soda Straw Small, hollow *stalactite* from which drops of water descend.

Solution Process by which a solid, liquid, or gaseous substance is combined chemically with a liquid or sometimes a gas or solid – a homogeneous mixture.

Speleogen Feature in a cave produced by *solution* of base rock.

Speleologist Person who professionally studies caves.

Speleology Scientific research of all aspects of caves.

Speleotherm Feature in a cave produced by deposits of mineral.

Spelunker Term applied to "cave buffs" – those who make a hobby of exploring and studying caves; different from *speleologist*

Stalactite Deposit of *calcium carbonate* (as *calcite*) resembling an icicle hanging from the ceiling or sides of a cavern, the result of deposition by dripping water.

Stalagmite Appears as an inverted *stalactite* growing upward from the floor of a cave caused by the dripping of calcareous water.

Townsend Big-eared Bat The bat most commonly seen in the Oregon Caves.

Vadose Water Water that seeps through the ground under the earth's surface and the water table.

Vadose Zone Region between the earth's surface and the water table.

Water Table Upper limit of the portion of the ground wholly saturated with water – meeting place of *vadose zone* and *pheratic zone*.

Bibliography

BOOKS:

Contor, Roger J. *The Underworld of Oregon Caves National Monument.* Crater Lake Natural History Assn. 1963.

Geographic Names Information System - Oregon U. S. Geological Survey. 1992.

Helbock, Richard W. *Oregon Post Offices 1847 - 1982.* LaPosta. 1982.

McArthur, Lewis L. *Oregon Geographic Names.* Sixth Ed. Oregon Historical Society Pr. 1992.

Peterson, Martin Severlin. *Joaquin Miller Literary Frontiersman.* Stanford Univ. Pr. 1937.

Sloane, Howard N. and Russell H. Gurnee. *Visiting American Caves.* Crown. 1966.

Turnbull, George S. *History of Oregon Newspapers.* Binford & Mort. 1939.

Walsh, Frank K. and William R. Halliday. *Oregon Caves: Discovery and Exploration.* Te-com-Tom Enterprises. 1971.

Watson, Chandler B. *Prehistoric Siskiyou Island and Marble Halls of Oregon.* Private Pub. 1909.

Webber, Bert and Margie. *Battleship Oregon, Bulldog of the Navy.* Webb Research Group. 1994.

_____. *Jacksonville, Oregon; Antique Town in a Modern Age.* Webb Research Group Publishers. 1994.

_____. *The Lure of Medford.* Webb Research Group Publishers. 1996.

_____. *The Siskiyou Line, Adventure in Railroading.* Webb Research Group Publishers. 1997.

PERIODICALS AND OTHER NON-BOOK MATERIALS

"A Terrible Tragedy in Depths of Oregon Caves; Frank Ellis … is Accidentally Killed." in *Courier.* [Grants Pass, Ore.] Aug. 6, 1909. p.1.

"Bat Rap" in *Oregon Caves Underworld.* Crater Lake Natural History Association. Vol. 6. 1993. p.3

"Caves Resort Ready to Open" in *Courier.* [Grants Pass, Ore.] Jun. 15, 1923.

Brown, Marcia. "Damage Totals Still Undetermined at Caves Chateau" in *Daily Courier.* [Grants Pass, Ore.] Jan. 28, 1965.p. 9.

Burch, Walter C. "Early Days of Oregon Caves" in *Illinois Valley News.* [Cave Junction, Ore.] Jun. 30, 1983.

Davidson, Elijah J. "History of the Discovery of the Marble Halls of Oregon" in *Oregon Historical Quarterly.* Vol. XXIII. No. 3. pp 274-276.

Fidler, William W. "The Josephine County Cave" in *Morning Oregonian.* Aug. 1, 1877. p.1.

_____ "An Account of the First Attempt At Exploration of the 'Oregon Caves'" in *Oregon Historical Quarterly* Vol. XXIII. No. 3. Sept. 1922 pp. 270-273. (This is a recap of the 1877 article 45 years later.)

Hahn, Barbara. "Workers Rediscover Hidden Cave While Repairing Monument" in *Daily Courier* [Grants Pass, Ore.] Jan. 25, 1990.

_____. "Renovation Brings Cave Back to Oregon Caves" in *Country Weekly.* [Courier Pub. Co. Grants Pass, Ore.] Mar. 15, 1995.

_____ "Oregon Caves Will Close For 3 Months" in *Daily Courier* [Grants Pass, Ore.] Nov. 12, 1996.

_____. "Oregon Caves Mapping Its Future" in *Daily Courier*. [Grants Pass, Ore.] Jan. 13, 1997.

Hill, Randy. "Natural Look Returns to Oregon Caves" in *Mail Tribune* [Medford, Ore.] Dec. 4, 1990.

"Josephine Caves Scenic Attraction; Portland Party Journeys to Southern Oregon" in *Sunday Oregonian*. [date missing from clipping]

"A Josephine County Cave" in *Morning Oregonian*. Aug. 1, 1877. P.1. *Josephine County Caves or the 'Marble Halls of Oregon' A Magnificent Labyrinth of Halls Located Near Grants Pass, Oregon.* [Booklet 1915].

Kadera, Jim. Limited Use Urged For Oregon Caves to Save Caverns from Tourist Hordes" in *Oregonian*. [Portland, Ore.] Nov. 7, 1971.

Michelson, Charles, "Another Western Marvel; Discovery of a Cavern in Oregon That Rivals the Mammoth Cave of Kentucky; The *Examiner's* Exploration of Many Miles of Chambers and Corridors Full of Beautiful and Curious Formations; A Week Among the Crevasses" in San Francisco *Examiner* Jul. 11, 1891.

_____. "Our Splendid Cavern, More About the Great Cave in the Northern Siskiyous" in San Francisco *Examiner* Jul. 12, 1891.

Miller, Joaquin. "Oregon's Marble Halls" in *Sunset*. Vol. XXIII. No. 3., Sept. 1909.

Millard, F. B. *The 'Examiners' Expedition's Further Discoveries on the Great Cave in Southern Oregon"* in San Francisco *Examiner*. May 26-27, 1894. *The Oregon Caves*. Siskiyou National Forest. U. S. Dept. Agri. nd [1924].

"Oregon Caves to Close for Renovation" in *Daily Courier*. [Grants Pass, Ore.] Jul. 24, 1985.

Oregon Caves National Monument Oregon Master Plan. U. S. Dept of Interior – National Park Service, 1975.

Oregon Caves National Monument; Draft General Management Plan and Environmental Impact Statement. U. S. Dept. Of Interior – National Park Service. 1997.

Oregon Caves Underworld; The Newspaper of the Oregon Caves National Monument. Crater Lake Natural History Ass'n. Vol. 9, 1994-1995; Vol. 10, 1996-1997.

"Oregon's Wonderland; Marble Halls–Devil's Slide and Bridal Chamber" in *Rogue River Argus*. June 10, 1915.

Reference Guide for Interpretive Programs; Oregon Caves National Monument.

June 15, 1923

CAVES RESORT READY TO OPEN

Grants Pass

Manager Sabin Says Things in Readiness for Today

The Oregon Caves resort will be ready today to handle all comers. states George Sabin, manager, who was in the city yesterday getting ready for the formal opening of the dining room and sleeping quarters, scheduled for today. Mr. Sabin states also that excellent dining room service will be provided, as Chef C. L. Smith has been secured for the season and is on hand today getting ready for the expected visitors. Mr. Smith is one of the most popular chefs who have been in Grants Pass and it is expected that many will make Sunday trips to the Caves and take dinner there.

In regard to the Sunday excursion of Cavemen to the Caves where they will be filmed by the Balmac educational film company, Mr. Sabin says provisions are being made for feeding and caring for everybody that will be there. Many are expected to be on hand to watch the filming operations and to see the new Caves resort after its opening.

"Oregon Caves National Monument National Parks Service." [Outline for guide's from which narratives are developed] 1993.

Roth, John and Steve Marks. *Oregon Caves National Monument.* Unpub. Ms. 1997.

Rowley, Dick. "A Trip From Grants Pass to the Limestone Caves of Josephine County; the Greatest Natural Curiosities of Oregon" in *Courier.* [Grants Pass, Ore.] Sep. 3, 1886.

Swofford, Jay and John Roth. "Names of Oregon Caves National Monument" in *Oregon Caves Tour Guide Manual* - Vol. III. 1990.

Williams, Ira A. "The Oregon Caves" in *Natural History* Vol XX. No. 4 pp-396-405. 1920.

Margie and Bert Webber with their "Field Research Unit."

About the Authors

Bert and Margie Webber have been writing and publishing books about the Oregon Country for over 25 years. They first visited the Oregon Caves in the early 1970's having heard about them as a peripheral to Bert's study of Gardner Cave near Metaline Falls, Washington.

Bert holds a degree in journalism from Whitworth College in Spokane, Washington. He is also a librarian having earned the Master of Library Science degree from studies at Portland State University and the University of Portland. Among several duties during World War-II, he graduated from Signal Corps Photographic Center operated at Paramount Studios, Astoria, New York. He has been a Commercial Photographer for more than fifty years. He has written well over one hundred newspaper and periodical features and spot news articles nearly all illustrated with his pictures. With his wife's assistance, he has written and illustrated over seventy non-fiction books.

Margie holds a Bachelor of Science degree in Nursing from the University of Washington and has completed some post-graduate work at Oregon State University. She served in many different nursing positions including school nursing, hospital, psychiatric and public health. As a young woman, she worked in a large photofinishing plant in Seattle, the third generation in her family to be connected with photography. For the books, she serves as an editor, a telephone communicator and frequently as a field photographer.

The Webbers live in Oregon's Rogue River Valley in the once-a-village, now the city of Central Point. Their home is about 85 road miles from the Oregon Caves. ⬦

Illustration Credits

Front/back covers: Nat'l Park Service

iii Author collection

iv National Park Service (NPS)

v Bert Webber

viii Oregon Dept. Transportation

14 Author collection

18 Bert Webber on
U.S. Forest Service map

19 Author collection

20-24 NPS

26-27 Author collection

42 Author collection

47 Bert Webber

48 Author collection

53 Author collection

59-61 Author collection

67 Author collection

70 Author collection

73-74 Author collection

76 Author collection

80 Author collection

82 Bert Webber

83 Author collection

84-88 Connecticut State Library

89-92 Author collection

93 (TOP / LOWER) Author coll.
(CENTER) Leonard G. Lukens coll.

94 Author collection

95 NPS

98-100 NPS

104 Author collection

105-106 NPS

108 Author collection

110 (map) NPS; photo Bert Webber

111 NPS

112 Bert Webber

114-115 Bert Webber

117-118 Bert Webber

120 Author collection

122 Oregon Dept. Transportation

123-124 Bert Webber

126 Bert Webber

128 (TOP) Author collection
(LOWER) Bert Webber

129 Bert Webber

130 Author collection

132 Author collection

133 Bert Webber

134 Author collection

135-140 Bert Webber

142 Author collection

143 (chart) NPS; photos Bert Webber

146-147 NPS

152 Author collection

164 NPS

182 Author collection

187 Author collection

190 Bert Webber

204 Oregon Caves Co.

207 Leonard G. Lukens coll.

209 NPS

217 NPS

218 Author coll.

280 O.C. Palmer collection

221 Oregon Caves Co.

222 (TOP) O.C. Palmer coll.
(LOWER) Bert Webber

223 Bert Webber

224 O.C. Palmer collection

225 Bert Webber

227 Bert Webber

232 Norman VanManen

239 Author collection

240 Author collection

Index

Page numbers in **bold-*italic*** type are pictures and maps

Names of caverns, grottos, etc., appearing in the "Names" Appendix are not included in this Index but are alphabetical in Appendix E p. 150ff. Such names appearing in this Index occur in the text on pages indicated.

110 Exit, *iv, 118,* 121, 129; discovered, 193; (map), *80*
acidic dew, 125
Aiken, Charles Sedgwick, quoted, 75
Anderson, H. V. permit declined, 198
Angle Falls Arch, *136*
animals, at caves, 32, 33, 95-101, 192
artist's work, *67, 70*
Baker, Sam, 15
Banana Grove, *129*; (map), *80*
bats, 32m, *95,* 96, 97, 100; bat gate, *99, 118*
Bear Pit, 82
bear stories, 98, 107, 149, 177
bears, 32, 33, 95, 96, 107, 192
Beauty Slide, 40
Beehive Room, 129
Beekman, Ben B., 141, 142
Beekman, C.C., 142
Bell Chamber, 69, 71
belly-squirming, *22*
Birdsey, Jim, 141, 144
Bisceglia, Gene, 150, 151
blackness, in cave, 50; *see also*: darkness
Bogie Room, 72
bones, animals, 32, 216
Bottomless Pit. 79
boxwork, 191
Bridal Room, 50
Brown, Lee, 150
Brownies Bathroom, 52
Budge, Ronnie Lee, as librarian, 16

Burch, Clair W., 145
Burch, John Wesley, 145
Burch, Walter C., *94,* 145, 147; mineral claim, 194; names passage, 158, names cavern, 162-163
cabins, built, 207; removed, 216, *see also*: cottages
calcite, 125, 131; crystals, *182*
California & Oregon Coast RR., *108,* 197, 200n
cameras, 50; how to use, 119
camp fire, *93*
Camp Henderson, 195
campers, 109
candles, Roman. 81
Captain Smith, 31; *see also*: Smith, Captain
carbide lamps, 205
carbide lantern, *see*: lanterns
carbonic acid, 46
Cardwell, W. W., 141
Carlsbad Caverns, 102
Cave Creek, *20,* 30n, 145; (map), *iv,* Christmas Flood, 150, its route, 156, named, 196, runs in Chateau, 210
Cave Creek Campground (map), *110*
cave interior (cutaway) *143*
Cave Junction post office opens, 211
Cave Junction, Ore., 109, 113, 151, 199; estab., 208; (map), *18, 110*
cave lighting, 179
"Cavemen," *204*; organized, 205
Cave Rafts, creation, 189

cave, creation of, 184-186; depths of, 9
Caves Highway, 151
caves, various others, 27, 43, 45, 102, 232
CCC, *See*: Civilian Conservation Corps
centipede, *98*
Chalet, 128; damaged (flood), 150, built, 205, 206, in 1998, *223,* m. 140
chapel (Joaquin Miler Chapel), *80*
Chapman, John M., early explorer, 193
Chateau, *218;* bedroom suite, *220,* completed, 210, damaged (flood), 150-151, fireplace, *221,* in 1930's, *220;* in 1940's, *104;* in 1998, *222, 223, 225*
children in caves, limitations, 216
children's services, 117
chipmunks, 95
Christiansen, Harry, 15, 140
Christmas 1964 flood, 15, 150, 180
Civilian Conservation Corps (CCC), 105-107, 158, 210
claustrophobia, 121
clay worms, 132, 191
column (sketch), *187*
columns, as walls, 40
Condon, Dr. Thomas, 141, *142,* 144; souvenirs, *143*
Connecticut State Library, 85
Connecting Tunnel, 127
coralloids, *see*: popcorn
cottages (cabins), *93*, 94
Craggies, wild cave, 200
Crater Lake Nat'l Park, estab., 197
Crater Lake Natural History Ass'n, formed, 212
crawlways, most eliminated, 205
Crescent City, Calif., 113; (map), *111*
Crystal Palace, 68
crystals, 68-69
Dale, Jimmie, early visitor, 192
darkness, *62,* 64, 69, 71; *see also*: blackness
Davidson, Carter, 17, 142, 144; as early visitor, 192, 193; his signature in cave, *21*

Davidson, Elijah J., as cave discoverer, 14, 17, 18, 78, *83,* 149, 192; as young man, *19*; memorialized, 14; monument to, *82*; returns, 193; with rifle *89*; with Rowley, *83*; m. 142n
Davidson, Winter, early visitor, 192
deer, black-tailed, *100*
Depression, affect on visits, 179
Devil's Backbone, 79
Devil's Kitchen, 52
Devil's Pass, 147
Diamond Hall, 147
Dining Room, 35
Doré, Gustave, 58
Douglas fir tree, roots of, 125
driveway 900 feet long, 19, 106, 219, *115*
Dry Room steps to, *126;* (map), *iv, 80*
Dunn, George W., 141
Eagle Room, 50
Elder, R. B., cave visitor, 52
electric light plant, built, 207
Elephant Chamber, 148
elevations, 20, 116; (in cave) (map), *iv*; Mt. Elijah, 9
Elijah's Cave, 10, 24
entrance (main) (map), *iv, 80, 86*
Examiner (newspaper), 12
Examiner artist, his work, *59, 60*
Examiner Expeditions, 26, 27-28, 29, 31, 37, 39, 40, 43-45, 48, 49, 52, 63, 132, 164, 193
Examiner explorations, 195, 196
Examiner party (cave visitors), 52, 56, 59
Exit 110, *iv, 118,* 121, 129; discovered, 193; (map), *80*
exit tunnel (map), *iv*
Exit Tunnel, 139, *140, 227*
Exit, old, *87*
Ferguson, Robert, 145
Fidler, Wm. F. as early explorer, 193; names the caves, 160
flashlights, in caves, *42, 118*
flood, damage, *see*: Christmas 1964 floc
flowstone (sketch), *187*

flowstone, 125, 127, *129*, 131, 165, 166, *190*; how created, 188

gasoline, 113

Ghost Chamber, 50, 51, 54-55, 58, 63-64, 82, 147; *see also*: Ghost Room

Ghost Room, 52, 55, 56-57, 131, *137*; (map), *iv, 80*; see *also*: Ghost Chamber

Ghost Room, type of rock, 181

Ghost's Hall, 44, 45

Giant's Tongue, 37

Gittings, J., cave visitor, 52

Godfrey, Endora ("Dora"), 19; her signature in cave, *21*

Godwin, Julius, early visitor, 192

Goodwin, Mrs. Julius, 19

Gordon, Dick and Kathy, 15

Grand Column, *73*, 131, *132;* (map), *80*

Grants Pass, 24n, 29, 50, 109, 146; (map), *18, 108, 111*

Grants Pass, as terminal for streetcar line to caves, 195

Gray Back Mountain, 142; *see also*: Grayback Mountain

Grayback Campground, 11n; cost of, 206; (map), *110*

Grayback Creek, 29, m.18

Grayback Mountain, 11n, 19

Great Limestone Caves, as name, 9

Great Oregon Caves, as name, 10

Guardian of the Cave, 36, 37

guide services (1930's), 92

guides, 113; certified, 109

Halliday, Wm., cave mapping proj., 214

Hanks, Prof. Henry G., 45

hard hats, 65n, 116, *118,* 121, 157

Harkness & Burch (adv.), *147*

Harkness Homer D., *94*, 145, 147; squatter's claim, 194

Harkness, Ernest, squatter's claim, 194

Harkness, F.(Frank)., 145, 146

Harkness, Samuel, 145

head, injury to, 57, 65, 116

Hearst, Wm. Randolph, 12, 25, 26, 196

Helictites, creation, 189

Hell's Gate, 146

Henderson, A. J., form Oregon Caves Imp. Co., 194

Henderson, Jack, 50

Highway 46 (map), *20, 111*

Hines, Bob, 150, 151

Holy of Holies, 82

Hornet's Nest, 148

Hot Room, 44

Illinois River, 29

Illinois Valley Visitors Info. Center, 109, *110,* 113, *114*; (map), *110*

Imagination Room, 127; steps to, *126*

injuries, in caves, 116; to heads, 57, 65, 116

jaguar bones, 103; discovered, 216

Jensen, as photographer, 72

Joaquin Miller Chapel., *73, 90, 133,* 161; (map), *iv*

John, David Jr., 19

John, David, Sr., 192

Johnson, Charles, 145

Johnston, T. H., permit not approved, 201

Jones, David, early visitor, 192

Joseph's Tomb, 82

Josephine County Cave, 21

Josephine County Caves, as name, 10

Josephine County Hist. Soc., 15

Josephine County, 24n, 28

Jules Verne's Well, *see*: Verne's Well

Kerby, Ore., 29, 31; (map), *108, 110*

Kincaid, John C., 71, 78, 79, 81; as cave guide, 196; names Watson's Gorge, 176; early explorer, 192, 193

Kincaid's Dance Hall, 82

King's Hallway, 52

King's Highway, 82

King's Place, 82

Knutson, Steve, 22, *23*

lanterns, 24, 50, 62, *73*; carbide, *24*

Last Chance Chamber, 148

lighting, 205, 208

Limestone Caves, 148

Livingston, Dr. David, 25

Logan Creek, 196
Luray Caverns, 27, 43
Mammoth Cave, 27, 28, 43, 72
Mammoth Chamber, 147
Mammoth Column, *74*
map, cave tour, *80*
maps, *iv, 18, 20, 80, 108*
Marble Halls of Oregon, 76, 91
Marble Halls of Oregon, as name, 10
Marks, Steve, 13
Mazamas mountaineers, visit caves, 202
McDaniels, Perry, 145
Meadow Mountain, 194n
Medford, Ore. (Map), *111*
Michelson, Charles, as reporter/explorer, 12, 25, 28, 41n, 49, 193
Michelson, Charles, *Examiner* Exped., 195
Millard, F. B., as reporter/explorer, 11, 48, 70
Miller, Joaquin, 13, *76*, 77, 78-79, 81; his enchanted horse, 161; names caverns, 155, 163, 165, 168, 169, 172-173, 174, 175, 177
Miller, Robert A., early explorer. 193
Miller's Chapel, 131; *see also*: Joaquin Miller Chapel
Mirror Room, 34
mondmilch, created, 190-191
Monte Cristo's Treasure Chamber, *53*, 64, 69
monument, to Davidson, *82*
Moses' Chamber, 82
Mt. Elijah, as name, 9, 167
musical stalactites, 171
Myers, Jefferson, 77; list of places visited (1907), 82
Nail, James, 193
Nat'l Mon. Proposed, 197
National Park Service, 113; obligation, 11; to manage Ore. Caves, 14
Neil, Frank R., 141
Neptune's Grotto, 102, 131
Niagara Falls, 82, *88, 122, 123,* 129,

131; (map), *iv, 80*
Nick's Bed Chamber, 82
Nick's Slide, 81
Nickerson, Frank., as guide, 31, 50, 52, 71, 78, 79, 106; lost in cave, 81; early explorer, 193, 194, forms Oregon Caves Imp. Co., 194; names cavern, 162
Old Nick's Bedchamber, 50
Ore. Caves as Nat'l Monum., *i, 14*; estab. 14
Oregon Agricultural College, 94
Oregon Cave, as name, 10
Oregon Caves (map), *18*
Oregon Caves Company, 15
Oregon Caves Improvement Co., 25, 26, 195, 219
Oregon Caves marble, formation of, 183-184
Oregon Caves Nat'l Mon. (map), *20*
Oregon Caves Nat'l Mon., plaque, *112*; (map), *110, 111*
Oregon Caves, as name, 20
Organ Loft, 69
Organic Act, 196
other caves, 102
Ouim, G. O., propose resort, 198
Palmer, Connie Baker, 15
Palmer, O. C, and Connie, 1984, *224*
Palmer, O. C. "Slug," 15
pamphlets, promotional, *84-88, 90-93*
Paradise Lost *90*, 82, 132, *134;* described by Miller, 79
parking lot, at caves, 206, 207, erosion to, 213
Passageway of the Whale, 125
Peck, Prof. Arthur L., 206, 219
Petrified Gardens, 125
photography in caves, 119
Pillar Room, 82
pillars, 68
Pinchot, Gifford, 196, 197
popcorn, 131, creation, 189
post office at caves, 206
post offices, Williamsburg, 24n
postmarks, *93, 207*

Princes' Boudoir, 52
proclamation (of President), *i*
Queen's Chamber, *120*
Queen's Palace, 148-149
Queen's Place, 82
Quinn, John O., cave visitor, 52
Rachel's Well, 82
Rainy Cavern, 41
rats, 101, 127
rental cabins, 128; cause damage to
      cave, 127
rental rates (1930's), 93
restrooms, *106*
Reynolds, D. B. as guide, 202
rimstone (map), *80*
Rimstone pool, 158
Rimstone Room, 159, 174
rimstone, *143*; creation of, 188
River Styx Bridge, *123, 124,* 125;
      (map), *80*
River Styx, 13, 30n, 44, 82, 121, 125;
      culverts, removed, 215; for drinking,
      151; (map) *iv*
road building, *91, 217*; to caves opens,
      203
road, 900-foot driveway, 106, *115,* 219
roads, *114,* winter conditions, 115
rock, classifications, 181-183
Roosevelt, Pres. Franklin D., 105
Roosevelt's Ride, 79, 82
Rose, Frank, 19; early visitor, 193
Roth, John, 13, 15
routes to cave, 11
Rowley, Dick, as guide, *74, 83, 120,*
      152, 164; hired as guide, 200, 202
Rowley, Dick, names caverns, 153,
      154, 155, 156, 158, 159, 160, 162,
      163, 166, 170, 171, 172, 176, 177
Rowley, with Davidson, *83*
RV (recreational vehicles), 11n, 109
Sabin, George C. Gen. Mgr., 93, 210,
      231
Scott, Rose M., 15
Scully, Helen, *22*
Shark's Jaw, 82
Shelfstone, creation, 189

Stanley, Henry M. explorer, 25
Star Chamber (The), 82
Stone, Col. L. D., cave visitor, 52, 63
Stone's Falls, 62, 64
Stygian (river), 13, 172, 174
Sucker Creek, 29, 30, 166, 195, 201
telephones (city), undependable, 203
telephones in cave, 211; *118*
temperatures, 115, 117, 121; in caves,
      43
Temple, Shirley, actress, *204*
tent houses, 205-206
tents, 94
Theatrical Stage, 82
Timeline - Oregon Caves, 192-217
toilets, public, installed, 203
Tomb of Rameses III, 52
tour group heads for cave, *112*
tour group in Ghost Room, *137*
tour route (map), *iv*
tours, guides, availability, 116, 119
trailers, 109
trails, hiking, 116n
tree roots, 125; (map), *80*
Unger, Jason, guide, 15, *118*
Univ. of Oregon Geology Museum,
      143
Van Manen, Norm, *123*
vandalism, in cave, 205
Veach, Robert, propose resort, 197-198
vermiculations, 191; *see also*: clay
      worms
Verne's Well, 59, 60, 64, 67
visitors at Nat'l Mnt., 178-180
visitors, at caves, 178-180
Voorhies, Amos E., 205
Walsh, Frank, 145
Washington's Statue, 82
water zones, 185
Watson, Chandler B, *14;*
      memorialized, 14; 77, 81; early
      explorer, 193; list of places visited
      1907, 82
Watson's Gorge, 82, 121; (map), *iv*
Webber, Bert and Margie, *232*
Webber, Bert, 75

Wedding Cake Room, 125, 135, 139
Whitworth College, 47, 232
Wigwam Room (map), *80*
Williams Creek, 19, 24n; as route to
    caves, 17, 18, 193, 194
Williams, Ore. (map), *18*
Williamsburg, Ore., 24
Windy Passage, 81
Wishing Post, 120
World War II affect on visits, 179
Worthington, Mr. (photographer), 25,
    40, 154
Zeverly, visitor, 72

This may have been the cabin mentioned on page 146 however there is no documentation provided with the picture.

Marble outcrop near caves' exit